'If you wa[...]
If you want to go far, go together.'

COFOUNDING
THE RIGHT WAY

A practical guide to successful
business partnerships

JANA NEVRLKA

COFOUNDING THE RIGHT WAY

First published in 2018 by

Panoma Press Ltd
48 St Vincent Drive, St Albans, Herts, AL1 5SJ, UK
info@panomapress.com
www.panomapress.com

Book layout by Neil Coe.

Printed on acid-free paper from managed forests.

ISBN 978-1-784521-24-0

The right of Jana Nevrlka to be identified as the author of this work has been asserted in accordance with sections 77 and 78 of the Copyright, Designs and Patents Act 1988.

A CIP catalogue record for this book is available from the British Library.

This book is available online and in bookstores.

Printed and bound in Great Britain by TJ International Ltd.

DEDICATION

To Leni

ACKNOWLEDGEMENTS

Before writing my own book, I never understood the purpose of the acknowledgements section. Well – now I do. As with so many other things in life, great things are scarcely, if ever, an individual effort. As an author, I learned by my own experience that without the great support, guidance, cheerleading, critical reviews and constructive feedback of others this book would not have happened.

And appreciating the collective effort I want to thank all the great people who helped along the way – directly with this book – or indirectly by shaping my knowledge and experience or being the role models on my path. Thank yous go to:

- To all my clients as working with their teams helped me to develop and fine-tune the 7 Cofounding Steps.

- To the Slicing Pie Family: Mike Moyer, Maxine Chow, Deborah Griffiths, Roger Rohner, Mario Erni, Jetse Sprey, Eric Kuenzi and Salvatore Iacangelo.

- To the Swiss Startups Club – the organising team with Anja Mihaldinec and Daniela Cerva – and all the members from whose stories I could learn.

- To the WYDR team – Matthias Doerner and Timo Hahn – who asked me to implement the first Slicing Pie dynamic equity split for their team in Switzerland and were kind enough to share their learning throughout its application.

- To the Balboa team – Paco Savio, Erich Zuger, Timo Klein; the Impact Hub team –Stefan Honnegger and Niels Roth, Daniel Leu, Rory Passey and many others who shared with me their cofounding stories and experiences.

- To Mindy Gibbins-Klein, the Book Midwife and Panoma Press team.

- To the beta readers for their invaluable feedback and expertise: Abhik Mukherjee, Christos Vakalopoulos, Dolly Delaney, Elvira Boeck, Fiona Flintham, Gareth Robinson, Karina Storinggaard, Katerina Klezlova, Lenka Nevrlkova, Nicole Menten, Rajesh Durbal, Richard Pemberton and Sascha Humbeli.

- Special thank you to:

  - Richard Pemberton for the multiple rounds and levels of support.

  - Nicole Menten for the input on team dynamics and organisational psychology.

  - Paco Savio and the Remolino team for the design gift.

- To all the great teachers of Rotterdam School of Management, Erasmus University and Masaryk University, especially to Prof. Dr. Roel de Lange, Dr. A. van den Brink, Prof. Dr. Ellen Hey, Ronald Poppe, Joep Elemans, Stef van der Velde and Julie Johnson.

- To my work colleagues whom I learned a lot from – Jiri Fiala, Emil Holub, Radka Nenickova, Martin Licenik, Edvard Rinck, Joost Vreeswijk, Alex Wijnen, Thijs Heijenrath, Luc Hautvast, Danny Loa, Krista Koeleman, Theo Elshof, Mudit Kapoor, Guillano Demon, Robin Errico and many others.

- To my previous business partners – for the successes and failures from which I learned so much.

- To my family without who I would not be who I am, get the chances in life I got – and have the courage to never stop learning, exploring and believing.

DISCLAIMER

I am a strong believer in looking at the big picture, solving issues holistically and combining knowledge across disciplines. This book summarises the main choices that you need to make as a cofounder and combines business, legal, finance and psychological insights and know-how. It is not meant to be a comprehensive academic guide in any of those disciplines; it is a bouquet selection of relevant bits and pieces that you, cofounder, can practically apply and use.

It is not possible to provide one universal formula that will be applicable to all. Nothing in this book should be interpreted as legal or tax advice; its objective is to raise awareness of the potential legal and tax issues that are inherent in business partnerships. It cannot and is not meant to provide individual legal or tax advice.

FOREWORD

Whatever you call them – cofounders, partners, employees or anything else – your startup team is simply a group of people trying to figure out if they can turn an idea and a vision into a real, actual business that serves customers and provides reliable cash flow. Unfortunately, people aren't perfect. As a species, we're pretty darn good at a lot of things, but we lack one essential entrepreneurial skill that would ensure our success: *we can't predict the future.* If we could, things would go a heck of a lot smoother.

Even the cleverest business idea and the clearest vision can't change the fact that the path to success, if it exists at all, is utterly unknowable. Sure, we can plan and project and promise and pretend we know what's going to happen, but even the brightest among us is going to be wrong. The only thing that never changes about a startup company is the fact that it's always changing.

When the changes come, relationships will be tested. Some people will rise to the challenge and move boldly forward, others will follow willingly and still others will cringe and recoil. Good feelings ebb and flow. Some people treat challenges as opportunities, some treat them as defeat. Even those with the best intentions can find themselves at odds with one another.

Cofounder conflicts are extremely common in startups and many are insurmountable ultimately leading to the demise of the company. Even the companies that do survive can be hindered by irreconcilable differences among founding teams. If your company is going to fail, it's better if it fails because your original idea or vision was flawed. If it fails because of founder conflicts you will be forever haunted by that gnawing feeling that it would have worked 'if only…'

What's interesting, however, is how easily conflicts can be resolved or avoided altogether. Choosing the right team and setting up systems that accommodate changes can allow founders to navigate start-up turmoil remarkably well. While there may be many reasons why your startup could fail, there frankly aren't that many reasons why your relationships will fail, and this book will help you mitigate problems as they inevitably arise.

In Chapter 6, Jana introduces Slicing Pie, an equity model I invented to help teams create a fair equity split in the face of extreme uncertainty. Over the years I've heard countless stories of not only how the model allowed the team to easily avoid equity split conflicts, but also how paralysing the process was *before* they found the model. Many made choices about equity splits that seemed logical at the time but ultimately destroyed their team and the company. The right equity model is one of those things that will not enable success, but the wrong equity split can easily lead to failure. The knowledge of Slicing Pie enables teams to focus on the factors that lead to success.

Throughout this book are concepts and ideas that can arm you with the knowledge you need to avoid common mistakes that well-meaning founders make all the time. Start-up teams can do amazing things with scarce resources. By leveraging the concepts in this book, you can set them up for success rather than facilitating their failure.

Jana and I have a common understanding: good teams can destroy good businesses because good people can make bad decisions. Many bad decisions can be avoided with the right knowledge. Your ideas and visions can put your people on the path to success, this book will help you keep them on it!

Mike Moyer
Inventor of Slicing Pie

CONTENTS

PREFACE – MY WHY

As I was growing up, the Iron Curtain fell and with that came many new opportunities, including opportunities for aspiring entrepreneurs. My father enthusiastically decided to start a consulting business with his brother. After a few struggling months, it was clear that the business would not work out. They could not agree on what to do or how to do it. It happens. Unfortunately, the result of the lack of common vision and suboptimal communication was not only the failure of the business, it also severely damaged the relationship between my father and his brother. The next time these two 'met' was at the funeral of my father's brother, after he tragically and unexpectedly died a few years later.

Now this story is a very sad one as death does not leave us many remedies. I did not realise until much later in my life how formative it was for me, the main impact in my own life being a strong tendency to avoid partnerships because of the potential damage the failure of partnerships can cause. And true, if you do not enter any partnerships you are not being exposed to the risk that they will not work out. But you are also missing out on all potential opportunities that a good partnership does create, as on your own you are always only the best you. And having partners – in life, in projects, in business – has real and tangible benefits... when it works. So luckily, I did not end there and kept trying. And the trying included quite a few failures with the gold nuggets of very valuable learnings in them.

Growing up in the Czech Republic (Czechoslovakia back in those days), I decided to become a lawyer so I could help to make the world a more just place. After getting my first two cum laude legal degrees in the Czech Republic, I continued studying European and International law in the Netherlands. At the beginning of my career, and after having worked as a stagier during my studies in the Czech Republic at the public prosecutor, law firm, NGO, court and

Ministry of Industry and Trade, I became very quickly disillusioned with how much I could achieve this objective by being a lawyer. After a short period as a corporate lawyer in Prague and following the flow of life, an interesting job offer and my private situation at the time, I decided to specialise in international tax law – in the Netherlands. Back in those days, I saw myself as a sort of modern-day Robin Hood and took a lot of pride in helping companies to optimise their taxes. I also learned a lot about business and about people as I was fortunate to work with companies across different industries and teams in most of the European countries. And next to my interesting job, I also completed a business degree. But after a while, I could not see so much value in what I was doing anymore.

For a while I tried to silence the inner voice which was pointing it out, but that strategy worked only for so long. Slowly realising that my biggest heroes were always entrepreneurs – you can tell a lot by looking at someone's library – I wanted to find out if I could be an entrepreneur myself. Not knowing where to start, I invested in a very early stage startup and for the first time in my life, I embarked on my first hands-on experience of having and running a business with a partner. In this project, it went kind of OK. I joined first as an investor then decided to become an active business partner as I wanted to test my entrepreneurial skills. After a few months working together, I took over the business as my business partner wanted to move on to different pastures and we could manage the whole process rather amicably and efficiently. What surprised me was how quickly the situation changed from building a business together to my business partner leaving. The only sticky point was the valuation of the business at the time and the buy-out price. Luckily, we managed the changed situation with no conflict, no damage to the business or relationship and no extra costs.

In my second business partnership attempt the story looked a bit different. Who said we learn more from our failures than from our successes? I assembled a team from two of my very close friends with whom I used to work in my previous consulting life to start a new business: focusing on standardising our knowledge in the area of law, tax and supply chain to provide one-stop-shop advice to startups. By that time, I realised that I wanted to work with and for entrepreneurs and wanted to use our knowledge to develop solutions – affordable and scalable – that would help them to grow their business internationally. It included development of online courses, templates and one-on-one consulting.

This partnership failed in two phases as we realised our commitment levels, personal situation, vision, willingness to risk and way of working were very different! Despite years of having worked together in the international consulting environment and years of being close friends, we did not have the knowledge we should have had – or obtained – prior to starting a business together. My motivation was to combine our knowledge to offer one-stop-shop advice, where normally the business owner would need to consult multiple experts with no guarantee that their advice would be compatible with each other's and which most entrepreneurs in the early stages cannot afford. However, looking even deeper, I mainly wanted someone else to buy into my vision and to do it together with me.

The first failure phase was when I realised that we could not agree on some basic rules of time commitment and translate our individual contributions in the suggested equity split. That situation quickly raised further commitment questions to one of the partners. From then on, it became clear quite quickly that for one of the partners the project was perhaps an interesting hobby and cool idea, but in no way a serious project that she could foresee as a next step in her career. This could have been fine had that been communicated clearly from the beginning. However, at that point the trust and relationship were already damaged and it did not make sense to continue our cooperation further. The exiting partner did kindly agree that we could use the materials developed – videos, webinar materials and templates – further.

The second failure phase was a few months later when I realised that the remaining partner was too busy with his consulting career and private situation, but most importantly so used to the consulting way of working that we spent more time discussing who should do what than actually doing things. Being back then already two years as an independent entrepreneur and out of the consulting world, I knew that you need to be ready to get your hands dirty. Unfortunately, the difference was so big and the progress so slow that despite the sunk costs, I realised it was better for me to accept the failure and move on.

As bitter and frustrating as it felt at the time when things fell apart – again – I was quite lucky as far as the material damage. The investment was limited to a few months of development work and a small amount of money. Still not pretty, but worth it for the lesson. On the personal side, one of the friendships was damaged beyond repair, the other one survived.

Looking back with the intention to at least understand which lessons I learned had two phases:

Phase one: blame the others – they were irresponsible, not transparent, not committed, did not understand that our business needed a different mindset and way of working. And they were the reason we failed. Well, that was the easy bit but not the complete picture.

Phase two: get the real learning. What have I overlooked? Which warning flags did I ignore? Was my motivation clear? Did I do proper due diligence and project plan? As you can imagine, this was the difficult bit. The confronting one. And the most valuable one. After stroking the hurt ego, I realised that the mistakes I made were quite a few: from my motivation to just not wanting to do it alone, to not checking with my business partners where they saw the business as part of their life and future career, to clearly agreeing everyone's commitment and the timeline for joining the business full-time. And not addressing the early warning flags when they were showing up late for our meetings and calls and somehow already in the beginning I felt that the project was priority number 10+ in their lives. I just wanted it to work and move on.

Alongside going through the first time entrepreneur rollercoaster and leaving my promising corporate career, I started to organise a networking and knowledge sharing platform for startups as I felt I needed a new network of people who were doing similar things and wanted to help all of us starting entrepreneurs and small business owners to learn from each other. And because of my background and experience, I got a lot of questions on cofounding and business partnerships. On how to do it right. On what to do when the founders disagree. On how to split the equity.

One day, one of the founders' teams asked me if I could help them implement the dynamic equity split model in Switzerland. I had a look at the model – being called the fairest equity split for bootstrapped startups – and I found it one of the best things invented after sliced bread. It was developed by an American serial entrepreneur after a few of his startups failed because of people issues. I started to look for ways to make it work in Europe and started to learn as much as I could about partnerships and how to make them work and last. And I still remember the surprise feeling from a) finding out how big an issue the failures in cofounding teams are in the real world and b) how little information is out there on the topic of how to build successful business partnerships. Also, the information that I found – and some of it undoubtedly very good! – would cover only selected specific aspects. There are business books on startup valuations, equity splits (most of them though do not include the dynamic equity split option), great books on some of the issues founders face, good materials on part of the soft side of business partnerships and the very helpful and practical *Slicing Pie Handbook* and other materials on the dynamic equity split. There is a summarised overview of the ones I found most valuable in the reference section of the Cofounding website: cofounding.info/resources. What puzzled me though was the absence of a holistic approach and advice.

And after selling my first business, while being busy looking for my purpose, the purpose found me. I continued to look for the better way in business partnerships. How we can work together, collaborate and create amazing companies – in teams – that will work, stay and win. I started to work with cofounders' teams to help them with the set-up of their teams – from how to work together to how to split their equity. Started coaching in startup accelerators on cofounding issues. Started developing the templates for the dynamic equity split in Europe and creating a network of European Slicing Pie lawyers and tax advisors. I realised that with the combined knowledge, experience and expertise I was so fortunate to collect I could provide most value in continuing working with entrepreneurs to help them to build cofounding teams that will win and last. From that I developed and fine-tuned a seven steps model on how to create a cofounding team and continue sharing the knowledge in every way I can.

At the time of writing this book I feel there is so much more to learn, develop and improve. And I realise that with every cofounding team I work with I learn some more. And from every war story I hear I learn some more. And I am also very much aware that the knowledge I am sharing with you now is by no means complete or final. My wish is to keep working and learning, and by sharing what I know now – helping entrepreneurs to cofound better. Today.

INTRODUCTION

Is This Book For You?

Are you either planning on, or in the process of, working with a team of cofounders in a business partnership? If so, then the answer is yes – this book is for you. It is a hands-on practical manual for business founders. It does not have as an ambition to summarise all the existing body of knowledge, nor to be an academic publication or legal handbook. It is a practical guide for you as a business founder to lead you through the steps on how to assemble and run your cofounding team. Arguably, the earlier in the process of selecting your cofounders and building your team you are, the better. That being said, especially in teams where communication, trust and openness – the main ingredients for working together – are present, you can also get a lot of value from fine-tuning the areas which might be suboptimal or verifying your equity split arrangement, as a few examples.

The first part of the book is structured around the seven steps of business partnerships done right and uses the steps to lead you through some of the main milestones and decisions in building your cofounding team. Going through the seven steps process will help you with some of the main questions that might be running through your cofounding head:

- Whether business partnership is the right choice for you.

- Identifying what you need to be looking for in your cofounders.

- How and where to find them and how to select the right cofounders.

- What do you need to know and understand about your potential cofounders before you seal the deal?

- What are the typical pitfalls and mistakes in cofounder negotiations?

- How to allocate the roles and responsibilities in your cofounding team?

- Which are the absolutely necessary conversations to have with your cofounders?

- How to split the equity between the cofounders.

- How to ensure that your cofounding team will stay motivated.

- How to ensure that your cofounding team will keep performing.

- What do you need to have in place to be safe from the legal point of view?

- How to document your cofounding agreement.

Some of the steps are fairly straightforward and common knowledge. For some others I have included an explanation of the main theoretical concepts – fixed and dynamic equity splits and vesting for example – so you will be making an informed choice on what is best for you. In case you are familiar with these concepts please feel free to skip them and stick with the process steps only.

The second part of the book deals with how to handle potential changes in your cofounding team, what to do if your cofounding team is experiencing troubles and how to correct it if everything in your current team is not right. It will help you to answer:

- What to do when one of the cofounders leaves.

- What is equity recovery framework and what do you need to have in place?

- Termination of a business partnership.

- What options do you have to solve conflicts and which one is suitable for which type of issues?

- How to correct business partnerships where the set-up is not right.

The purpose of this book is to give you – the founder – the information and the tools. It starts with the awareness about what you need to pay attention to. Then it gives you the knowledge on how to deal with the decisions ahead of you, which options you have, what do you want to consider and how to implement it.

Why Should You Be Interested?

The sunny side of business partnerships

What is so powerful about business partnerships? Sharing a dream, vision, purpose (fill your words) is one of the most powerful things people can do. And countless studies – from psychology to sociology to anthropology – are over and over confirming that we are a social and collaborative species. (Business) partners are people who get together to create something together. Something that is bigger than just the sum of their individual contributions. It is joining resources and sharing risks for a relatively uncertain future outcome. It is jointly creating something new.

Multiple studies have confirmed that partnerships have a higher chance to create sustainable companies. To create faster growing companies. To be more innovative. To be more creative. To be more stable and resourceful.

Do you know how many out of the top 10 most valuable companies worldwide according to their market capitalisation in 2017 were founded by solo founders? Three. The myth of the 'uberfounder' who founds and grows unicorns by himself is largely overrated and the truth is that most successful and fast-growing companies are founded and grown by teams.

Most valuable companies in the Fortune 500[1]

RANK	COMPANY	INDUSTRY	MARKET VALUE ($BIL)
1	Apple	Computers, Office Equipment	534
2	Alphabet	Internet Services and Retailing	507
3	Microsoft	Computer Software	413
4	Exxon Mobil	Petroleum Refining	326
5	Facebook	Internet Services and Retailing	321
6	Berkshire Hathaway	Insurance: Property and Casualty (Stock)	312
7	Johnson & Johnson	Pharmaceuticals	288
8	General Electric	Diversified Financials	271
9	Amazon.com	Internet Services and Retailing	250
10	Wells Fargo	Commercial Banks	242

Source: S&P Capital IQ

Synergies - one plus one is more than two

Done right, there are powerful synergies to be created in a team by joining resources, knowledge, brains and hearts that go way beyond what anyone can achieve on their own. We seem to have an idealised notion of the lonely solo founders who built an empire from nothing. If truth be told though, they rarely did it by themselves in all the stages and they are more of an exception that confirms the rule. Building a successful business requires a combination of skills and resources that are very seldom found under one hat. Being on your own also means that you are always the smartest person in the room and there is no one to check or question your decision. From creativity to innovation, teams produce consistently better results most of the time. Another very practical consideration is workload

---

1 Gandel, S. (2016, February 04). 10 Most Valuable Companies in the Fortune 500. Retrieved July 20, 2017, from http://fortune.com/2016/02/04/most-valuable-companies-fortune-500-apple/

and capacity. With joining forces, not only is there a pool of different skills, expertise and strengths, but also a very practical amount of hands who can do stuff. And in today's business world, being able to move fast can often mean the difference between success and failure.

For the ones that get it right, the 1+1 can equal much more than 2.

Shared risks and responsibilities

But it is not only a simple business principle of adding resources. There is the psychological side as well. Emotionally, functioning partnerships provide an additional level of comfort to know that the risks are shared too. And not only that, from motivation to perseverance the chances are that the team is stronger than any single individual. Anyone who has been through the journey of building a business knows how demanding it is. The stage is full of uncertainties, high pressure and limited resources. Depending on what it is that you are trying to achieve, it can also be full of people telling you that it is not possible. To keep motivated, strong and performing for a single individual is a very demanding task. The benefit of the team is that, combined, the chances are there will always be someone in the team able to keep up the motivation as the going gets tough.

From a potential investor's perspective, team versus solo founder is a very important aspect they look at. If all their investment is hanging on a solo founder it is by definition a much higher risk than if the venture is backed by a strong team.

The death rate

Typically, most successful and fast-growing startups would have between two and five cofounders. Because whether it is the skills, different perspectives on the team or keeping the spirit when the going gets tough, a good team will always be stronger than the best solo flyer. Having a good functioning cofounding team is very directly and strongly increasing the chance of your business succeeding and access to investors should you need them. Some venture capitalists that I interviewed would even go as far as to say they do not invest in the idea but in the team.

Founding a business as a partnership looks from this perspective as a no-brainer, does it not? Well, yes and no. Because as much as it is possible and preferable to create strong cofounding teams, it is not easy, and if done blindly, the risk of getting it wrong is very high.

> ## "People problems are the leading cause of failure in startups."
>
> Dr. Noam Wasserman

According to several studies – from statistical data mining to empirical investors' observations – up to 65% of startup failures are being attributed to problems within the cofounding team.[2] It is not the wrong idea, lack of capital or access to clients. It is the people! With the scary death rate of business partnerships, depending on the source, being between 60-70%,[3] the risks of business partnerships going wrong is alarmingly high. Even higher than the modern marriage failure rate. And the costs of the high failure rate of business partnerships are enormous.

---

2   Wasserman, N. (2012). The Founder's Dilemmas. Princeton & Oxford, USA: Princeton University Press
3   Lehavi, D., PhD (2015). Business Partnership Essentials. Los Angeles, USA: Dorene Lehavi, PhD

Business risk

Any potential instability in your cofounding team – whether it is the tension between the partners, not being able to perform as a team, unresolved issues or decision deadlock to name a few frequent ones – are significant risks to your business. The uncertainty and tension becomes very quickly obvious to your employees and potential partners, and also slows down or stalls your business growth and can deplete the resources you need for growing your business. Slowed growth or partial loss of resources is still the better case scenario. The other end of the spectrum is the cemetery of failed businesses. Because despite a few famous examples where the business flourished and grew despite the cofounders' dispute (Facebook being probably the most notorious example), the majority of businesses with cofounder issues were never heard of because they did not survive.

Relationship risk

Depending on how you resolve the conflicts in the cofounding team, the risk is that it will cause damage to your underlying relationship. Especially if that is in the blurred zone where the cofounder has an additional social link to you – be it a friend or a family member – this risk is very significant. If your partnership happens to be in the majority of failed partnerships category, some of the closest relationships in your life could be damaged, as was the case in my father's failed consulting business with his brother – beyond repair.

Lost opportunity risk

It is very common for founders who had a negative cofounding team experience (direct or indirect) to decide against partnership as the safest way to mitigate the risks. And while partnerships are certainly not a universally best option, they do have in most cases a stronger potential than solo founders. So the hidden costs of people not partnering further because they do not know how to make it work is a significant missed opportunity.

The Seven Cofounding Steps

Next to the philosophical question of why are we so disastrously bad in partnerships, the practical question is: can we do something about it?

The answer is yes, we can. It starts with awareness. That we should not expect and assume that we know how. What do you think would be a failure rate for first timers jumping with a parachute without previous experience or instructions? Somehow, there are very few of us who would even think of jumping from 10km high without a parachute or with a parachute that we do not know how to use. I believe it is mainly due to that fact that the fatality rate for skydiving is even less than the one for car driving – below 1%. It is because we are aware that before trying to do that we should first learn how.

"This is so cool ... Leonard's moved into jump position without his parachute. Let's see how long it takes before he realises that it's missing."

However, we consider it completely normal to enter partnerships – whether private or business – without learning about the pitfalls and mitigating the risks. And yes, I would wish that we would have more knowledge. And that our education system, given the importance of cooperation in human species development, would teach us how to create and maintain successful and fulfilling partnerships. But the fact is that our knowledge – theoretical and practical – on the partnership topic is very scarce and frustratingly insufficient. As the death rate unfortunately confirms.

Many founders – mainly first timers and especially in the 'rose-tinted glasses' period typical of the beginning of the relationship – do not think about it. And yes, starting your own business requires strong belief and optimism. However, believing that you are simply the fortunate one and that your business partnership will be automatically and without any consideration in the surviving minority of business partnerships is not optimistic. It is delusional. The serial entrepreneurs most of the time know this as they have been burnt before. They know about the risks, but still not necessarily how to mitigate them.

The good news is, with awareness and knowing how to mitigate the risks, your chance of building a lasting and performing cofounding team is much higher. Similar to the parachute jumpers, once you know what to do and how to do it, the scarily high chances of failure of business partnerships does not have to be your nightmare. And as most probably you are starting to build a business to realise your dreams, and not your nightmares, it does make sense to give it some attention.

I strongly believe that the rather bleak perspective of only about 30% of business partnerships going right can be much improved. In the category of the failed partnerships there are certainly some that just did not have a chance to make it, but there are many that would either not start or would have lasted if done right.

So how to do it right? Combining my own experience and expertise, listening to many cofounding stories gone wrong (and occasionally some gone right), working with many cofounding teams and researching everything I could find out there, I believe the secret is in realising how important a decision you are making when deciding to cofound a business with someone else and then following logical steps, in the right order, to do it right.

I am the first to admit that there is always a limit on how much standardised formulas and processes can capture the uniqueness and magic of any interaction between individual people. And it is important to keep that in mind. And I also strongly believe and have seen in my practice that following the outlined steps helps to avoid the most common pitfalls and significantly increases the chance to choose the right cofounders and build a team that will perform and last. The smartest way – with respect for the unique and individual – is to follow a formula that works, especially when it comes to such an important building stone of your business as your cofounding team is. Because between all the urgent and important priorities competing for your attention and resources, you need to realise:

Get your cofounding team right and you will be in the best position to handle all the changes, uncertainties and intense times ahead. Get it wrong and not even the best business idea has a high chance to survive.

The seven steps of business partnership done right are the result of the combined learnings and knowledge to help you get it right.

7 steps of business partnerships done right

01 Confirm if partnership is right for you

No	Don't know	Yes
↓	↓	↓
Found solo	Take the cofounder test	Continue to step 2

02 Know what you are looking for

>> Start with your business plan
>> Map the gap
>> Find the best way to fill the gap
>> Fill the gap

03 Preselect cofounders

>> Confirm that everyone is a true cofounder
>> Understand yourself and your cofounders
>> Check essential partnership ingredients
>> Align common purpose

04 Dating times

○	○	○
Working styles	Personality differences	Try before you buy

05 Get serious

○ Roles and reponsibilities
○ Relationships
○ Conversations to have

06 Split the equity

#1 Decide on equity split   **#2** Split the equity
>> Dynamic split
>> Fixed split ⟨ Equal
                Unequal

07 Cofounders agreement

>> Document it
>> **LIVE IT**

2017 © cofounding.info

How To Use This Book

The book is structured around the Seven Cofounding Steps – from confirming if partnership is right for you to selecting the right cofounders, splitting equity and implementing the cofounding agreement – all in Chapters 1-7. All the failed business partnership war stories I came across can be linked to either skipping one or more of these steps or doing them in the wrong order.

The second part deals with how to handle change and conflict in your cofounding team, and lastly how to fix your cofounding base in case there are some wobbly parts.

Some of the chapters have quite a bit of explanation of the theoretical concepts; we will touch upon different equity splits options, startup valuations and explanation of main conflict resolution mechanisms for example. In case you are familiar with the concepts, please do feel free to skip. Without the ambition to be encyclopaedic on issues related to cofounding, I did try to provide an overview of the main concepts for ease of application.

As you hold this book in your hands, I congratulate you on significantly increasing the chances of building the right team and making it succeed! With knowing how, anything is possible.

 CONE ICON Exercises: are included to help you to do the steps correctly. Yes, you can skip them to move faster. You do get more value from the book and the process though if you complete them.

 BULLET ICON Checklists: before moving to the next step, make sure that you completed all the required actions. Remember – shortcuts are the longest possible ways to achieve your goal.

BOWLER ICON Case studies: are used to illustrate the points on real life business cases; you do not need to make all the mistakes yourself – sometimes it is much better, faster and cheaper to learn from the mistakes of others.

 PAGE ICON Templates and resources: reference to the templates and resources included on cofounding.info. Of course I want you to go and check all the other awesome material that can help you, which is regularly updated on the website. The main reason for having it there is that as the resources are updated and further developed, by checking it on the website you will get the latest up-to-date materials. The section also provides further materials and reading on the business partnership topic if you want to go deeper into any of the respective subtopics.

Terminology

Throughout the book I had to make some choices that I believe make it more readable and understandable material. They include:

He/she: gender equality being very close to my heart, the absolutely correct way to refer to an individual cofounder would be he/she. Being correct, I find it cumbersome for the reader, so in the wish for more female cofounders, I opted for she. For all the male readers and cofounders, I hope you will kindly accept and know that it also means he!

Entrepreneurs/startups/small business owners: these are all very different categories and there are many discussions on definitions and abuse or overuse of these terms. I use them interchangeably throughout as this book is about business partnerships – be it for high-growth startups or small business owners. The principles of business partnerships are the same.

Cofounder/partnership/shareholder agreement: depending on which phase the business partnership is in, the absolutely correct way would be to refer to the business partnership agreements prior to incorporation of legal entity as partnership agreements and after the incorporation of either the limited liability company or public company as shareholder agreements. To make it easier for you as the reader I use the term cofounder agreement to cover both and only make the distinction when it is really relevant.

Cash amounts: as cofounding and business partnerships are global – the currency in the examples is left blank – to enable you to fill whichever currency you think in.

> ## "An investment in knowledge pays the best interest."
>
> Benjamin Franklin

CHAPTER 1:

PARTNERSHIP YES OR NO?

Common Partnership Disqualifiers

I appreciate it might sound a bit odd to start to read about business partnerships with the question whether it is right for you. But believe me, as much as I do believe that together we are stronger than alone, I also believe that one size does not fit all. And that if partnership is not the right answer for you, you will do yourself – and the others! – a big favour to know it earlier rather than later.

Typical disqualifiers that might indicate that business partnership is not the right choice for you or in your current situation include:

You have all the essential resources to get the business going by yourself

If that is the case and you are considering business partnerships it might be either because you do not *want* to do it by yourself or you *prefer* to have a team. I would strongly recommend you to consider other ways to address your needs (more on the options later) than business partnership as it might not be the most suitable option for your situation. Whether it is the need for team, or support, in case you really do have all the resources, adding employees or creating a network of mentors and ambassadors could be a better solution to address your needs. As much as having business partners could be very powerful, if you do not really need them, you might not be in the best position to really use it, and having a business partner next to the benefits also adds complexity. Always. So if you have all you need, consider moving by yourself.

You prefer to keep full control of the business

There is no way around this one. If you prefer to keep full control of your future business, you are best positioned to remain a sole shareholder. In cofounding teams, even if you remain the majority shareholder, you will lose part of the control of your business. It depends a lot on the legal set-up and your cofounding agreement; some decisions in your future business might (legally) require unanimous decision (of all shareholders), some might need qualified majority or some could be done independently by any shareholder. It is not possible to explain all the potential scenarios in this section; to a large extent you can determine it by choosing the legal form of your company, voting rights and decision-making rules in your cofounding agreement. The fact remains though that once you include other partners in your business you no longer have full control of it.

You are not a team player

Without any judgments attached, knowing yourself is the best starting point. And if you know you are not a team player, you might do much better by growing your team with employees rather than cofounders – more flexible, much clearer hierarchy and no need to push the square peg through the round hole.

If you answered yes to any of the above points, I would strongly recommend to you to think again if you do want to proceed in a business partnership. It is better to consider carefully before getting involved with a business partner then realising later that it was actually not the best course of action and reverse it.

Examine Your Motivation Carefully

> ## "Founding decisions need to be made by design, not by default."
>
> Dr. Noam Wasserman

The next stage starts with knowing your motivation first. Why is it so important? Because knowing your motivation helps you to decide whether you are entering the partnership for the right reasons. Understanding your motivation for wanting to have cofounders is also an essential prerequisite for choosing the right ones. The most common motivations include:

You need additional resources

You cannot do it on your own; you are missing some critical resources which could be:

- Human resources: skills, experience, expertise, ideas, hands.

- Social resources: access to networks.

- Financial resources: cash or other assets.

Examining your vision – or even better, a concrete business plan and mapping the gap between what you have and can provide and what you are missing – is the way to identifying if and which additional resources are needed. This process also applies for existing teams in need of expansion.

Once you have identified what you need, the next step, *before* moving on to look for a cofounder who would have these resources, is to evaluate if finding that resource in the form of adding a cofounder is your best option. It can be that outsourcing, getting a volunteer or buying that resource is more suitable. Or that you can obtain it in a different way – for example an external loan instead of exchanging part of your equity for financing from an investor or cofounder. Similarly, sometimes a faster and more flexible way to access the needed resource is by collaboration or joint venture (which is a much more independent way of working together, frequently limited in time and to a specific project and without creating a joint legal entity).

Mapping additional resources is explained in more detail in the next chapter.

You want to have a team

Theoretically you do have all the required resources to start by yourself, but you are well aware how difficult it is to do it on your own. It could be that you prefer to work in a team. Or that you feel isolated when doing things on your own. Or that you prefer to share the risks. Or have the feeling that someone else being willing to develop your idea with you is the additional confirmation that you are looking for.

If your main motivation is in this category, please pause and re-evaluate. Is there another way to address your need? Many misplaced founder's choices tend to come out of this category. The reason why you are looking for the cofounder does not clearly specify what the cofounder should deliver to the business. Unless you combine it with adding a cofounder with a resource that makes sense from the business viewpoint, you are actually looking for a cheerleader. And sooner or later the choice of adding a cheerleader as a cofounder will backfire as it is neither right for you nor for the 'cheerleader' cofounder. In the many failure cofounding stories, many come out of this category.

There needs to be more understanding of why someone would join your cofounding team – from both sides. If you do not have that or clearly define it, these partnerships are typically not only the least stable ones but also the ones that are quite complex to dissolve as very often neither the motivation nor how the partnership should have worked was addressed upfront.

The strongest motivation being not to do it alone blurs the selection criteria for the future cofounder because if your main motivation is not to do it alone, pretty much anyone would do. It is also a very strong factor contributing to ignoring warning flags as you have less clarity on what you need to evaluate in your future partner because you simply only want someone to join your dream. Remember that there are other ways to address the emotional needs of this motivation – be it by getting a mentor, coach, advisory board or independent network of partners. Or create a team by hiring employees or getting on board enthusiastic volunteers and ambassadors, not cofounders.

You are looking for (innovation) synergies

Especially if your future business aims at creating something new – be it a new product, service or a new way to deliver an existing one – innovation is typically born on intersections and from diverse teams crossing between different areas of expertise, cultural backgrounds or points of view. Diverse teams are known to be more likely to innovate. Or maybe you are looking for any of the other known benefits that cofounding teams are known to deliver – if done right – be it shared responsibilities, better decision making or spreading risk.

 One of the most successful – in terms of innovation, growth and maximising diversity – teams that I had a chance to meet is the Balboa cofounding team. They managed to create a gym for people who like to work out but do not like gyms. This is in my words. In theirs – they created an urban community which provides sustainable fitness for the mainstream population in a way which is fun and addictive. They do not have members. They have fans. In an industry which is highly oversaturated but oh so repetitive at the same time, they managed to progress from a ghetto garage next to Zurich main station to three prime locations in two years and with an international expansion coming next. What was their secret? They are all great guys. And as much as we are used to seeing examples of the synergies in sports and music, they managed to combine their individual strengths and very different backgrounds, personalities, expertise and way of working into one of the most functional and inspiring teams I have ever come across. Is there anything further apart than Swiss ex-banker, Argentinian artist and German IT specialist turned fitness trainer? When interviewing their team it was very interesting to see how much they were aware of each other's strengths and differences, and managed from the beginning onward to maximise the use of the diversity and at the same time use each other's strengths.

And witnessing how powerful such a diverse team can be in creating something truly new, I also will admit that making it work is an art (which can be mastered) and not commonplace.

External factors

Being pragmatic, you might be aware that whether it is to participate in some of the excellent accelerator programmes or to get external funding, cofounding teams are preferred to solo founders. This being a valid motivation, in order to work it still needs to be executed properly, by choosing the cofounders that will bring the additional valuable resources and choosing the right ones. Because whether in business or in life, it is better to be solo than to be in the wrong relationship for the sake of being in a relationship.

Checklist

- I am sure that business partnership is the right choice for me.

- I am fully aware and conscious of what is my main motivation for business partnership.

KNOW WHAT YOU ARE LOOKING FOR

After this chapter you will know:

- How to identify what you are looking for.

- Cofounder's story on (correcting) Step 2.

- How to find cofounders.

- Considerations on cofounding teams – how many and how diverse.

The process to define what you are looking for is fairly simple – what is important is to follow the process:

Know what you are looking for

>> Start with your business plan
>> Map the gap
>> Find the best way to fill the gap
>> Fill the gap

y What You Are Looking For

your business plan

ng team composition starts from your vision. eady identified resources that you will need according to your business plan, not the other way round. I am not insisting on having a 100-page document with every little detail planned out. I am insisting on having a very good understanding of what your business strategy is going to be and to be able to define which resources you need to start and grow it. The term resources will be used in a broad context to include skills, experience, expertise, industry knowledge, access to networks, intellectual property and cash. At this point, you will benefit from being as open to feedback as you possibly can. Do find the experts in the field to talk to and get their feedback. Similarly, do find entrepreneurs who have been there before and get their feedback. How good your planning is will be to a large extent determined by the number of potentially uncomfortable conversations you are willing to have. I understand you. The entrepreneur dream at this stage is fragile. It is a newborn idea. You do have the tendency to protect it. However, showing it to people who might have a useful input and being willing to listen to their input and adjust at this stage can save you a few pivot rounds later. And remember, it is you who decides which feedback feels right and you want to integrate and which not. Being able and willing to ask for it and listen is the beginning.

There are also successful examples of reverse application. Successful companies that started by the team coming together and wanting to build a business together, and starting with brainstorming on different ideas before choosing the one to go for. It is possible. If you want to go this way, I still recommend you to start with an inventory of the skills and assets that you have and look for complementary resources in your cofounders: different backgrounds, expertise, experience, access to networks or skills.

If you are into a healthy and tasty lifestyle, you have probably heard of Innocent Drinks. Rich, Adam and Jon, the cofounders of Innocent Drinks, had met during their studies in the early 1990s. Becoming friends, they went on a snowboarding holiday during which they decided to stop talking about starting a business and actually start one. They brainstormed several ideas before coming up with the smoothies one. After spending six months working on smoothie recipes and £500 on fruit, the trio sold their drinks from a stall at a music festival in London. People were asked to put their empty bottles in a 'yes' or 'no' bin depending on whether they thought the three should quit their jobs to make smoothies. At the end of the festival the 'yes' bin was full, with only three cups in the 'no' bin, so they went to their work the next day and resigned. In 15 months they were able to bring the product from idea to market. The majority stake of the company was eventually acquired by the Coca-Cola Company.[4]

For the majority of cofounders who start with an idea and want to create the team to help them realise the idea, the next steps are mapping the vision/business plan against the available resources. The other way is to first create a team and then together develop the business idea to work on.

 We will use Kim's story to illustrate how the process is applied in practice. Kim is a strategic marketer, a purpose economist and a businesswoman, who is driven by advancing gender equality and who wants to build a company that would address the issue by using finance as a vehicle for change. She starts with the business plan that identifies that one of the solutions could be to build an

---

4   Innocent drinks. (n.d.). Retrieved July 21, 2017, from http://www.innocentdrinks.co.uk/us/our-story

investment platform allowing ordinary people to invest to support the gender cause while making a profit. Based on her business plan, she develops the following inventory of resources that she needs to get to the proof of concept.

Skills	Experience	Expertise	Cash
• Strategy • Business development • Financial forecasting • Networking	• Startup CEO • Early stage business development	• Investment advisors industry (input) • Financial markets industry (output)	• 100k

Stage 2: Map the gap

Imagine you are planning a trip: you need to decide how you will get to where you want to go, make the travel arrangements, find out what the weather will be like when you get there, sort out what you will need for the trip, from travel insurance and vaccinations to the things you want to take with you. And then you know what you already have and what you still need to get. This step is very similar. Once you have decided where you want to go and when you want to be there, you do exactly the same: in the resource category you mark what you already have and what is left are the resources that you need to add.

 Back to the example of Kim's startup – Kim now critically evaluated which resources she has and highlighted the ones she needs to acquire:

Skills	Experience	Expertise (must get)	Cash (prefer to get)
• Strategy • Business development • Financial forecasting • Networking	• Startup CEO • Early stage business development	• Investment advisors industry (input) • Financial markets industry (output)	• 100k for the first stage

Stage 3: Evaluate what is the best way to fill the gap

Once you have a clear picture of what you need, you want to evaluate what is the best way to get the resources. There are always several options and a responsible and informed decision includes looking at all the options you have and deciding which one is the best one for your future business.

The options to consider include:

- Getting on board cofounders who have the needed resources.

- Get the missing resources yourself – for example acquiring new skills or knowledge that you need.

- Outsourcing: paying for the resources that someone else has – typically this would be an expert knowledge that you only need for part or in some stage of the project.

- External financing: if available in your case, you might consider getting a loan (instead of an investor).

- Volunteers: there are many people who would like to participate in interesting projects and startup ventures and have valuable skills and resources to offer and are happy to do that in exchange for the experience or for the purpose of being part of something they believe in.

You can find as your starting point skill share platforms overview in the resource section on cofounding.info.

Ambassadors and mentors: if you are looking for access to a network or specific niche expertise that is needed only for some stage, you might want to look in your network and recruit for your project ambassadors and mentors who believe in your idea and would like to help you.

In Kim's case:

1. In the 'must get' category is:

   a) Investment advisory industry expertise

   b) Financial markets industry expertise

As this is expertise she does not have and it is a core resource for her business plan, she has the following options:

   a) Acquire the expertise herself.

   b) Find people who have that expertise and buy that expertise – as consultants.

   c) Find people who have that expertise, get them on board as cofounders and 'buy' their expertise for equity in the business.

Evaluating the options shows:

   a) Acquiring the expertise herself is possible, but she will need a lot of time and practical involvement. This option will take too long and is very demanding on her time and focus; as she wants to move the concept forward now, not a good option.

b) External consultants – as this is a core skill and it is before proof of concept, this is potentially a very expensive option and it is not clear that she could get the involvement and motivation that she needs.

c) Cofounders – in this case and given that it is core skill, this is the preferred option.

2. As the 'nice to have' category she identified the 100k cash, the options she has are:

a) Ask all cofounders for investment – she needs to find out if the cofounders do have and are prepared to invest in the business.

b) Get external funding – in the form of a loan or convertible loan or equity; this option might be very difficult to get in such an early stage of the business, unless coming from the common three Fs: family, friends or fools.

c) Invest the funds herself – this option is the riskiest one for her.

Evaluating all the options, it seems that option a) ask cofounders for investment is the best option, with the second alternative to invest the funds herself.

Stage 4: Fill the gap

Make sure that the cofounder option is your best option. It might not feel like this at the start, but the equity of your business is valuable *and* a limited resource. It is possible, and does happen frequently, that as you progress through the business development stages, you identify additional resources that you need – whether expertise, knowledge or cash – and you want to make sure that you have an 'equity buffer' left to use for acquiring the additional resources if need be. Advisable is also to ring-fence part of your equity pool for future key employees. Therefore, if there are other options to get what you need than exchanging it for equity, try hard first with these other options.

Now you not only know which resources you need, but also that finding a suitable cofounder that has the resources is your best and preferred option. Only now are you ready to start looking for the suitable candidates! Similar with looking for anything else, unless you know what you are looking for it will cost you much more time, and the chance that you will end up with something other than what you need is very high! This is a relatively minor risk when we speak about your summer holiday shopping, but a much higher risk when choosing partners for one of the most important relationships in your life – your cofounding team.

> # "You don't build a business. You build people. And then people build business."
>
> Zig Ziglar

Write a Future Cofounder Job Description:

i. Specify the required education, experience, skills and characteristics.

ii. Link back to your business plan and confirm that with adding such a cofounder(s) you will have all the essential resources.

iii.   Keep the cofounder job description and before making your final decision on inviting a cofounder to join your team, check it against the list.

Cofounders Story On (Correcting) Step 2

To illustrate the importance of Step 2 applied timely and correctly – one of the cofounders I had the chance to work with – and whose case study was helping to explain Step 2 in the previous Section – was kind enough to share her journey from her own – the cofounder's/ CEO – perspective.

'Easter 2017 I sat on holiday with my partner who was challenging me: "I am sorry, I do not see that you are moving forward, it seems like you go in circles and are still unhappy." It hurt to hear the words, but he had a point.

I knew what I had to do. I had to follow my dream and build a startup. I had been starting other initiatives as compensation, but what I really wanted to do was build a startup. A startup in the fin-tech area, with the goal to advance gender equality by using finance as a vehicle. I knew it was crazy, would be tough and require a lot of stamina. It was a big risk.

I made the decision. I had to – if not for me, then for my family who did not deserve to live with an unhappy and restless person. I decided then and there to apply for the fin-tech accelerator programmes as a next step. I had the idea for more than a year, I had a Google folder full of plans and documents and I knew that the deadlines for applying for two very well-known fin-tech accelerator programmes were only weeks away. I needed to act very fast, to get people on board, to make a pitch, a business plan and a first prototype.

I knew I needed a team for two reasons. I am a team person. I always was and do not enjoy working alone. I played football, not tennis, for a reason. The second reason was that the accelerator programmes require it. I had tried to get people to jump on my idea, but it had never really happened, which is one of the reasons I had not pursued it and instead went with other ideas and jobs. This time was different; I could no longer afford not to follow my real dream. Doing this startup is what I want, no more excuses. So this time I was concrete when asking people to join. I asked three people to join.

I called a colleague/friend of mine, who shared the same passion and vision as me regarding gender equality. She is an incredible smart woman, with lots of energy and she knows how to get things done. We had worked together for years in a female networking organisation and complimenting each other excellently. She had herself reached out to me earlier, so when I called her and explained to her my plan, she said yes. I was so happy and thrilled she did that. I was convinced we would be great together.

I called another woman, with 20 years plus of industry experience. We had recently gotten back into contact and had played with the idea and spent hours discussing the importance of moving money in finance in the right direction, yet still did not know each other that well. We had a very strong connection from the beginning and saw eye to eye on what we wanted to change in the finance world. I wrote her an email asking: are you in? She had to think about it, meet to discuss the vision. She said yes after our conversations.

The third person I called, was the CEO of the company where I had worked the last four years and still do some work. He is the CEO of a digital mobile agency building the most amazing digital mobile apps and businesses. I know they would be a great technology partner and we had been talking about this since the beginning of my idea. We had never done it before, because he and the agency would not be my day to day partners and sit 1200 km away. Again, being a footballer, I needed a team fully committed with the same passion on site. We agreed to keep talking, to help each other but wait with the details before I was clearer what I was building, since at this point I only had an idea, vision and a lot of passion. Time might tell that we did not need their exact competences.

So in a few days, I had a team. Two local partners and a technology partner I could call on, when the time came. None of them had ever met each other when agreeing to be a part.

Work started. We now had 10 days to submit the first application for the fin-tech accelerator programme. We all worked hard, mostly during evenings as we had other commitments. As we pressed 'submit' late on a Friday evening, we had all still not met in person. We had had some disagreement, but we had sorted it out and with the mind-set 'we are under a deadline, let's just get it done'. We were in a production mode, in a startup mode. It worked, we did produce some good material. The second application process started and we did the same thing. Through this process we got to meet and we got to know each other better. My experienced partner started to question the younger partner more frequently. She was primarily asking about what exactly she was going to do. I did not understand it at the time and thought she was being too sensitive. I was also frustrated that she could not articulate her concerns more specifically so I asked her to trust me and give the younger partner more time. She did, but the feeling did not go away. We had been in production mode for a month filling out applications or doing pitches for the jury, we even spent two days in a boot camp. We worked brilliantly together on stage. We did what we needed to do for the sake of the company. We all had an eye on the ball. Getting into the accelerator programme.

Next thing I knew, I heard the words, "you made it, you are one of the finalists." These were the words for the renowned fin-tech accelerator programme, F10 of Zurich. I could feel the joy throughout my entire body. I turned around, hugged the experienced partner who was with me at the time, the program manager, the mentor that I had not yet spoken to and the other startup who had delivered us the news.

Wow – we did it. It felt just great.

And then came shit, oh no, what did I do? I am not sure I am ready for this. Can we do it? Can I do it? It was similar to having a positive pregnancy test in your hand. So much joy, it is what you really want, but boy, what a responsibility. Excitement coupled with fear. Suddenly our startup was real. Until we heard those words, it was as if it was not really happening. Now it was. It existed. Before, it was ideas, words.

Something else made me rather uneasy: did I have the right partners? I was not sure. All of a sudden the questions from my experienced partner came up. I started questioning, is she right or is she too complicated? I had let the issue pass, but could feel it, feel it when we were together, feel I was not behaving 100% myself, which in itself is a warning sign. Something was off. All of a sudden I was consumed with this question. Building this startup was a dream coming true and we were building something together and I was the one carrying the baby this time. I needed to ensure the best possible start which does not include unresolved issues or bad feelings in the cofounding team.

It had been a long journey and now I was going into an official relationship with other people – not forever but in my head for at least a five-year period and we were going to bring the child into this world together. When realising this, I again started thinking shit, what did I do, how could I have been so careless?

I knew why. I wanted it so badly that I had brought two partners on board without giving much thought to which competences we needed or considerations as to whether the team would work well together. I thought having a common vision, growth mindset and willingness to work hard was enough. I thought I am good with people, we can make it work.

It had worked. We had made it into the programme. Yet it was not quite right for making a cofounding team.

1. On the competence side, we were missing key skills such as CTO, finance backend and legal. This did not worry me too much because I had access to these and would be able to activate them when the time was right. But at the same time, I had brought in one person whose competences we did not need at the start, my younger friend who was amazing at building a community, which we also needed, but only down the line. It was a poor fit for the time being.

2. On the people side, I was building a strong culture and somehow it did not really work beautifully with the three of us. It is hard to explain, but it was in the air and I could feel it. Lots of this came from the competence misalignment and complication of being three, with different ways of communicating, experiences and reasons for being part of the team.

I had been blind. I had not seen the competence problem as big as it was. I thought the culture part was more important and was so convinced we would make a dream team. But we did not. I had tried to solve it by being the middle man and organising around it. A skill I had learned from working in political organisations and being a consultant. So, it comes naturally to me. But it was a mistake. I made a big mistake and when I realised it, it was too late to solve it. It had come to a point where I needed to decide between the partners or find a new partner altogether.

The initial problem came because of lack of clarity of what is needed in the startup phase and due to my blind spot for my friend who shared my passion and who I had worked so well with in other settings.

The second problem came trying to solve it behind the scenes. Because I had not realised the big picture I had not been able to bring it to a meta level. In hindsight, it is clear. My younger friend would have been an excellent first strategic employee once we were bigger, but was not a typical co-founder in fin-tech. I had my fear of doing it alone, my personal need for energy drove my decision doing the hours where I needed a team.

It did not work how it should. It should not have been this complicated, and I had to decide, choosing either of my partners or choosing a third person. Decisions like this are never easy. I chose the experienced partner. Might seem easy on paper, yet, nothing is that simple, because she, like me could also have handled the issue differently and I still did not know her that well. I really appreciate both people, they are both incredible. On top, they both had played a role in getting this venture off the ground, something I will always be thankful for. Yet, sometimes, it just does not work and you as an entrepreneur need to fix it.

The choice came with a price, hurting a friend I had worked well with for years. Even if we were not best friends, I still considered her a friend. It was very hard. I let her down. Not intentionally, but it happened anyway. I believe you always have a choice and not choosing is also a choice, very often the worst one with time. So, I did what I thought was right.

I must forgive myself. It would have been easy if this was just business, but it does not mean you do not feel the pain and the guilt of causing pain to others. I know we will be fine with time although something might stay broken. I could have handled it differently and hope I will in the future.

Here are the learnings I took with me:

1. Use gut feeling *and* rational analysis.

2. Spend some time on the rational analysis, which competences do you really need in the team. Especially, if you come from the business side, it is very easy to end up with too many business people, but not enough people who can execute/produce. For example I have a MSc in Business Administration, specialised in marketing and 10 years' experience in running international marketing departments, but I am not a copywriter, graphic designer, or marketing producer. Be careful not to have too many managers. We had that, but were missing the production power.

3. Date some more and make sure all potential cofounders date. I was too much in the middle and created small silos. I should have insisted on spending more time together all three, talking about values, vision, mission, no-go's and expectations. Somehow, I had that individually with both but we did not all three share it. Note, I did not add the technology partner in on these conversations at this point because I saw them more as partners, not cofounders. Meaning, they have critical skills we need. It might be these skills will be paid with equity, but it might be these are paid with cash. There is an excellent fit between us, but they are not cofounders.

4. Do not play the political person behind the scenes, trying to solve the situation with diplomacy. I should have taken it much more face on with all three in the room earlier. When I got the two to talk together it was too late. Take the bull by the horns, even when you do not understand it completely, but if you feel it, it exists. You might have people who do not feel it as intensely as you, but they also need to take it seriously even when you cannot articulate it. This part I need to train for the rest of my life. I am assuming, if you are a more rational person, that this can seem like a teenage drama. It is not, it is real and it is an advantage to learn to have these conversations. Like point one; use feelings and rational analysis.

5. Spend time on the soft stuff, the people, the values, understanding motivations. Some might say it is over analysing, but rather do that in the beginning. Do not accept that there is no time for this stuff, because you will constantly be busy, so you need to prioritise it. Again, I spend time on it, but not collectively. When we were the three together we were in production mode. This is dangerous. You risk, like in my case, to damage relationships and, in the end, not addressing it early will cost you more time and resources later.

6. Make the tough calls. Sometimes you cannot fix things, sometimes it is just not right: timing, chemistry, others. Then do not just keep it. Make the call. Even if I could have done a lot of things differently, at the end I made the call, no dragging things out.

7. Work with and look for experts and guidance. I spoke with some very experienced people from the startup environment; people who had built their own startups and experienced failures on the way and startup advisors. They confirmed the importance of culture, underlined the need of competence fit and the danger of diluting equity by bringing too many people in too early. Working together with the cofounding expert helped me to identify what the issue in my initial team was and what is the right corrective action.

8. Forgive yourself. You make mistakes, learn, own up, stay human. Under no circumstances put it under the carpet. I have learned to forgive myself, but I will just never be good at this.

In sum, solve it, do not shy away. Be ready for feelings, good and bad. Being a cofounder is not just a job, you are starting something more personal, riskier, with more at stake. Once in, it is more difficult to leave, so spend time on the people stuff and the rational stuff. A common vision is not enough –– so many parameters must fit. For instance, we still miss core competences and are still considering how to best bring them onboard.

That being said, if you want to do it, do it, do it with a partner. In my experience it is ten times better than alone, but then again, I have always preferred football to tennis. Listen to your gut, listen to your head and listen to your heart.

'Go get them and sweep them away.'

How To Find Cofounders

Congratulations, now you have a clear picture of what you are looking for! Ready for the next step, which is where do you find them? Again, wanting your business to have the highest chance to succeed, it is important not to speed through this phase and make sure that you identify and select the *best*, not the immediately obvious or available candidates.

There are a few avenues to explore. For all cases do not limit your search to only one of them! As nicely put by Stefan Honegger, a very experienced startup expert from the Impact Hub in Zurich: 'Sometimes the best cofounders are people you would never think of.' So be open. And look everywhere.

Your friends

This is an obvious pool and one that is at your fingertips. It is also a very frequently chosen one. And it can work. However, there are a few words of caution before you select from this one.

Yes, one of Kim's friends used to work as an investment advisor 20 years ago – now does that make her the best possible candidate to fill the industry expertise gap? It does make her a candidate, but the chances are if Kim keeps looking, she might potentially find better suited candidates. So, wanting to build the strongest team possible, she should not stop here.

Risk of being too confident on knowing your friend well

With friends (and family), we often start with the assumption that we know them well. And hopefully we do – as friends (or family members). Very often though, we imagine that we know each other much better than we actually do. There is a whole world of difference between spending your Sunday afternoon barbecue with someone while talking about the meaning of life and getting them onboard as your cofounder. The context between social interaction and high pressure startup business development is quite different.

Because of the (often misleading) familiarity, you might feel less need to do a thorough due diligence than you would with a stranger. But you should be even more conscientious with your due diligence on a friend because of the tendency to overlook that comes from thinking that you know them so well. In the case of my failed partnership, the part that I knew about my friend – the tendency to cut corners and operate sometimes in the grey zones – amused me privately. In the business context I found it slowly but surely deteriorating our mutual trust.

Risk of avoiding sensitive discussions

Because of the existing connection, you might feel less motivated to discuss potentially 'sensitive' issues, like equity split or required commitment, and just feel happy that your friend likes your idea. This is a very important warning flag. Assuming your friend is the best possible cofounder for what you are looking for, you need to be able to add to the existing friendship relationship the professional cofounding one – and to be able to discuss all aspects of the business openly and respectfully. If you aren't able to, do not move further until you fix it. No exceptions. You would not hire even a cleaning lady without specifying when she works, how many hours and what it is that you expect her to do. Inviting someone to join as a cofounder is a much deeper commitment than hiring a part-time or full-time employee. And you are offering part of the equity in your future company in return!

Risk of avoiding documenting your agreement

Another common tendency with friends (and family) is the tendency to rely more on trust and less on documenting the agreements that you made. Again, there is no reason to let the existing social relationship change the reasonable business owner ways of working.

Additionally, unlike when you start working with strangers and you co-create the ways of working together, cofounders with existing previous (social) relationship have to uncreate the prior relationship first. This is similar for family or ex-colleagues (if the context is different).

Despite the enormous popularity of choosing cofounders from existing social relationships (friends and family being a very frequent pool), after the honeymoon period, teams with prior social relationships tend to be significantly less stable.[5]

So remember: these cofounding relationships can work, but unless you do the proper due diligence and follow all the steps as you would do with a complete stranger, they just rarely do. And because of the tendency to think that you know and the danger of existing assumptions, you should actually pay even more attention than when going through the process with complete strangers.

---

5   Wasserman, N. (2012). The founder's dilemmas: anticipating and avoiding the pitfalls that can sink a start-up, p. 103. Princeton, NJ: Princeton University Press

> ## "A friendship founded on business is a good deal better than a business founded on friendship."
>
> John D. Rockefeller

Your family members

The pool of family members, similarly to the pool of friends, is a very frequently used one. Also for similar reasons, it is the one that is close to you, you think you know your family members well, there is even higher pre-existent trust and you have a good picture of the resources they could bring.

All the caution points from the friends category apply here similarly:

- Risk of being too confident on your knowledge about the family member.

- Risk of avoiding sensitive discussions.

- Risk of avoiding documenting your agreement.

Additionally, in case the business partnership does not work out, be aware that there is a risk of damage to the underlying social relationship. In case of friends this is a very severe risk, but the intensity can be further multiplied if the cofounder is a family member.

For managing the partnership, you also need to be sure that you either feel comfortable or can outsource (if you have more cofounders) potentially sensitive decisions such as:

- How do you fire your brother?

- How do you address with your mother-in-law that she is underperforming?

- If your startup CEO happens to be your girlfriend, how do you keep the working disputes outside your bedroom?

Proper due diligence, making sure that you can create the business relationship next to the existing social one and have open conversations about sensitive issues, as well as documenting your agreement, are the necessary mitigation measures to address the increased risk of this pool.

Your classmates

This is another very interesting pool to definitely explore because you might have valuable insights into the skills, ways of working or attitudes from your common student times. Do keep in mind that the context is still different (yes, you did work together during your MBA on that real-life case study and there is still a difference if that case study is as real as your own business, savings at risk and feeding your family) from the outcome of this 'case study'. Depending also on which studies you did together, it is important that the cofounder satisfies the resource requirement; if you studied together, you might likely have similar backgrounds and expertise. It is important to double-check if you are really adding a cofounder with resources which you need and not just someone who you know and feel comfortable to work with.

Your ex-colleagues

Here you are even closer in having insights into the skills, ways of working and attitudes as you used to work with your ex-colleague before. What you want and need to check properly is if the resource which you are looking for is a skill or knowledge which a) is transferable and b) will fit in the new context.

In my failed business partnership, both of the selected cofounders were my ex-colleagues. After a few months of a rather painful and frustrating business development phase, the project failed. My due diligence mistake in step 2 was on both levels: transferability of the skill and new context fit:

a) Transferable resource: we used to work together for an international strategic consultancy where the majority of our clients were large multinationals. With developing know-how products for startups we struggled with the different mindset and approach that our new target client group required. I realised that as knowledgeable as my chosen cofounders were in their respective field of expertise, they were not able to adapt the knowledge and use it for a different client group.

b) Team fit in the new context: similarly, the working style which is very accepted and somewhat functioning in a large consulting firm is not fitting at all for a lean startup, where you need to get your hands dirty and do a lot of the stuff that you are used to outsourcing yourself.

You can certainly find valuable cofounders from your ex-colleagues. However, as with the friends and family categories, the deemed familiarity and basis of the relationship actually requires you to pay even more attention when doing your due diligence and going through the process. Mistakes are more likely to happen to us when we think we know.

 Simon and Andreas used to work together in an investment bank. Then their paths separated until one day they decided to join forces and start an investment fund together. In the meantime, Andreas' career developed more in the expert/public relationship direction, where he was a frequently cited and sought after expert to comment on the developments in the financial market. Simon, on the other hand, developed his career in a more entrepreneurial way. He gained his first entrepreneurial experience by building a 25+ employees financial advisory firm which he sold three years later. When starting the next business, together with Andreas, their initial assumption was that they would be equal partners. Luckily, after our initial session with both partners they decided to re-evaluate this assumption and wait. A few months into running the joint business it became very clear that it is mainly Simon who is driving the business – from the set-up of the business to providing the initial investment, to first clients acquisition. Andreas' role and value in the new context – startup investment fund environment and requirements are quite different from public relationship expert of an investment bank – still remains to be proven. They continue working together and grow the business despite the initial assumption on equal contributions being different. In this case, thanks to deciding to first work together to test their initial assumptions, they did not have to reverse early decisions on equal equity split – either by negotiating a buy-out or in the worst case scenario where they would not agree, by terminating the business. A better solution in the case of Simon and Andreas would have been to agree an initial probation period to test their individual contribution without indicating an initial equal equity split assumption. It is human nature that we are somewhat more ready to accept to work towards a dangling carrot than having the carrot promised and then taken away from us. From a psychological/team stability/ relationship point of view this would have been a better solution.

Social networks

There are many opportunities to connect with people through various existing social and professional platforms and networks. Chances are that someone you know might know someone you need and it is recommended that you use the power of your networks, be it LinkedIn, Facebook or your alumni's networks.

You want to 'go public' and start communication only once you know what it is that you are looking for and the more specific and accurate you are in your description, the better chance that your connections could help you. The exercise to write a cofounders 'job description' comes in handy here. If you are not specific enough, you might end up meeting with many potential candidates who are actually not what you are looking for.

Skill share startup platforms

There are many people who would like to participate in interesting projects and startup ventures and have valuable skills and resources to offer – and lack the big idea themselves.

 You can find as your starting point skill share platforms overview in the resource section on cofounding.info.

Networking events

Depending on the resource you are looking for, it could also be interesting to check networking events in your neighbourhood:

By specific topic

Industry or technology – for example if you want to start a business based on the block chain technology, you will definitely want to attend the events organised about block chain developments. You might find your future cofounders among the event participants.

By interest area

Entrepreneurship is hot. The events for entrepreneurs or 'wanna-preneurs' – the folk in transition who are flirting with the idea of entrepreneurship – are mushrooming.

A good starting point is:

- Chamber of Commerce events.

- Local universities events.

- Ask your entrepreneur friends for the networks they are part of.

 You can find as your starting point entrepreneurs events overview in the resource section on cofounding.info.

Serendipity

And then there is serendipity – the phenomenon of finding interesting or valuable things by chance. And believe it or not, a few of the very successful cofounding teams I saw would swear by using this avenue. So talk. A lot. To random strangers. About your idea. And you might be surprised how one hint leads to another. This one is recommended to do in parallel to the others anyway. Be it for the feedback, be it for the unexpected connections or simply for sending the message with your idea out there. I am very aware how first-time founders especially are afraid that people might steal their idea and would like to sign an NDA (non-disclosure agreement) with anyone. If I may share an observation of a few years in the startup scene: ideas are worthless. There you have it. They are. I know it is little bit of a harsh truth and I am not saying that your idea cannot become in the future extremely valuable. But in the beginning, ideas are worthless. A few special cases and industries are an exception – biotech or IT for example. But they are exceptions. And even in this case you do not need to disclose the (patent pending) invention to talk to others about what you are looking for in your cofounding team. What any seasoned entrepreneur or investor will confirm to you, the value only comes with executing your idea. So please – go ahead and talk about yours, to anyone who is willing to listen. And keep your eyes and ears open for what comes back.

What Else To Consider For Your Cofounder Team

Did we already speak about the one size does not fit all? That is not only true for who is the best cofounder for you, but also what is the ideal mix. There are, however, some golden nuggets of wisdom that you can consider when deciding what the ideal cofounder mix is for your business.

How many cofounders?

Apparently, in the opinion of VC or serial entrepreneurs, the ballpark recommended range is between two and five cofounders. However, the answer to this question should be primarily driven by the needs of your business.

You can go back to the exercise where you mapped your business plan to define the required resources that you need and deciding that the best way to acquire them is as cofounders. The golden rule is to look for cofounders that are the best candidates and combine most of the resources that you need. It might not be obvious in the beginning, but each new cofounder exponentially increases the complexity, coordination costs and communication needs of your team. You are balancing two objectives: a) fill all the required resources with the best candidate and b) do it with as few people as possible.

Homogeneous vs diverse teams

Have you ever travelled in Thailand? My favourite saying of all the 'original' products street sellers proffered is 'same same but different'. As confusing as it sounds at first, it is the ideal description of a great team. Your team should be partly 'same same' for the vision, motivation and ambition, and partly different in respect of the skills, approach, backgrounds and ways of thinking.

We all have a tendency to hang out with people who are like us. It is so much easier. If you choose this easy way in forming your cofounders team, you will be able to move faster at the start – less time needed for alignment and figuring out how to work together. And you will probably have easier decision making as you will tend to gravitate towards the same solutions. However, in this way you might be missing out on some of the greatest potentials of partnerships which is to have different opinions, skills and talents. Teams with diverse backgrounds tend to be in general focused more on facts and process the facts more accurately, and to be more creative and innovative.[6] Next to the human capital difference, there is also the social capital diversity. Cofounders with different backgrounds tend to have access to different networks. Additionally, a common risk with cofounders of similar backgrounds is overlapping roles and wanting all to do the same.

It is a balancing act. Teams on either side of the spectrum – extremely homogenous or extremely diverse – are scoring less on their collective intelligence[7] than balanced diverse teams. The extremely homogenous teams are running the risk of suboptimal decisions while the extremely heterogeneous teams are running the risk of too slow decision making and storming over performing.

---

6   Grant, D. R. (2016, November 04). Why Diverse Teams Are Smarter. Harvard Business Review, Retrieved July 21, 2017, from https://hbr.org/2016/11/why-diverse-teams-are-smarter?referral=03759&cm_vc=rr_item_page.bottom
7   Malone, A. W. (2014, July 31). Defend Your Research: What Makes a Team Smarter? More Women. Harvard Business Review. Retrieved July 29, 2017, from https://hbr.org/2011/06/defend-your-research-what-makes-a-team-smarter-more-women

There is no right or wrong – just know that while there are short-term benefits of homogeneity, there are also long-term risks. And choose what fits your business best, not what is the easiest thing to do at the start. The right mix will very much depend on your industry, vision and need for speed.

Checklist

- I have clarity on which resources I need to execute my vision/business plan.

- I confirmed that the best way to get the required resources is by adding a cofounder who has them.

- I have a clear specification on what I am looking for – cofounder job description.

- I checked all possible pools for the best potential candidates for my future cofounders.

What am I looking for?

Capital . $$$

Resources - Business backgroun...
          - Knowledge

PRESELECT YOUR COFOUNDERS

Preselect cofounders

>> Confirm that everyone is a true cofounder
>> Understand yourself and your cofounders
>> Check essential partnership ingredients
>> Align common purpose

You know that partnership is right for you and you know what you are looking for. The next step is to choose the final candidates for your future cofounders. The due diligence aspect is a very strong one. We often spend hours researching our next holiday destination or which gadget to buy. I cannot stress enough how important it is to go under the surface and get to know your cofounder candidates before you commit. Do not go to bed with the first date.

In this chapter you will learn:

- What are the essential elements to qualify as a true cofounder.

- What you need to understand about yourself and your prospective cofounders:

- o Beliefs

- o Values

- o Motivation

- o Drivers

- o Context

- o Personalities

Useful scenario exercise – to test the cofounders' understanding and learn about your potential team dynamics.

What are the essential ingredients for a functioning business partnership.

Confirm That Everyone On The Team Is A True Cofounder

When assembling your cofounding team, you expect your cofounders to bring resources, commitment and willingness to take risk. The combination of all these three elements is crucial. Unless all the three components are present, the chances are that you either have outsourced consultants or early employees – and you do not want to make the mistake of involving them as cofounders – to share the equity and control of your company with them.

Resources

Running the risk of being repetitive, make sure that it is clear to you and also to the cofounding candidate which resources they are bringing to the party. You can use the human, social and financial resource categorisation to help you to define it:

- Human resources: skills, experience, expertise, ideas. → Business

- Social resources: access to networks. → Knows hamptons

- Financial resources: cash or other valuable assets. → 💰💲💲

Needless to say, the cofounding candidate not only needs to clearly know what she is expected to bring but also to confirm that she can and wants to contribute the required resource.

Commitment

You want to have the commitment of your cofounders defined – both the starting commitment and the ongoing one. You do want to speak about how much commitment over the course of time are your cofounders not only willing but also able to invest in the business. Be as realistic as possible, knowing that life always has surprises in store.

Full-time commitment of all cofounders from the beginning

This is the easy one as all the cofounders commit their full-time availability from the beginning to the business. It still makes sense to speak about how you will work together – if you plan to get an office or expect to work from a client location or from home office. And how much flexibility – geographically and time-wise – your cofounders need and expect.

Part-time commitment

Frequently, some of the cofounders will have day jobs or other projects on the side and for various reasons (typically financial) need at least some time to handle multiple commitments simultaneously. The more radical approaches strongly recommend full-time involvement, in the spirit you are either on the bus or off the bus. And yes, if that is possible for all cofounders it clearly is the preferred option as it enables the team to move quicker. But it is also possible to build a successful business with a cofounders' team where, temporarily, not all cofounders are involved full-time. The important element here is to clearly define the commitment of the part-time cofounders, together with clearly defining the time frame and/or milestones when they will join full-time. Transition is sometimes helpful to get the business off the ground by bootstrapping instead of looking for external investment early on. However, unless all cofounders have the intention to join the business full-time they might not be all true cofounders. And I did experience cases when, through discussing the commitment, the parties early on realised that they should not continue the cofounder team formation but rather look for alternative ways to work together for the benefits of all.

When defining commitment, you want to discuss both the resources (for example time – being x amount of hours a week) and availability (which days of the week, are weekends on or off, evenings?) so that you can plan. Later when we speak about roles and responsibilities, the commitment definition will be very important for the whole team to be able to evaluate, and correct, how the cofounders are performing and potentially how to deal with underperformance.

Willingness to take risk

This is probably the most important aspect that distinguishes cofounders from (early) employees, based on the principle that cofounders invest their resources with the expectations of future reward. That means that they are putting their resources at risk; if the startup succeeds they will be rewarded (and hoping for a multiplication effect) but if the startup fails they will lose their investment. It can be the cash invested to get the business started, the time the cofounders work for the startup or any other resource that they bring. Unless the cofounder is taking a risk, they are not a cofounder but could instead be an early employee or an outsourced consultant. You can still decide to share part of the company equity with them, for motivation. However, the amount of equity that you would share with an early employee could significantly differ from a cofounder and it is also important to keep in mind that you are not only sharing the future profit potential of the company but also the control over it.

 Peter and Paul decide to start a travel agency specialising in holidays that combine travel and personal development – from yoga retreats in Ibiz, to survival camps in the Amazon. From the beginning, Peter took the leading role and care of incorporation of the company, provided the funds for the starting capital and got the first clients, generating positive cash flow in the first three months. Paul, to support the business, moved with his family to another country where Peter incorporated and operated the business. He did not invest any personal funds in the business and started receiving a salary from the third month onwards.

Question: Is Paul a true cofounder?

Resources: Paul is working full-time for the company since the beginning.

Commitment: Paul is committing his full-time work and has relocated.

Risk: Paul has two months' outstanding salary which will be paid later and no other financial investment in the business.

When working with Peter we analysed the situation and by considering these three elements it became clear that Paul is more likely an early employee. Peter can still decide to increase Paul's motivation and loyalty by giving him some equity in the company. However, given the fact that the risk that Paul took is limited to two months' outstanding salary to be paid later, Paul is not a true cofounder. Relocating his own family is comparable to Paul relocating his family for a new job, within a probation period.

 Marianne, Philip and David started an accounting firm. Marianne is from the beginning full-time involved in the business development, and invested 80% of the required cash. Philip and David each provided 10% of the needed capital and commit five hours a week to work on concrete client projects. Philip and David agreed to join the business full-time when there will be enough projects for each cofounder to be paid their fair market salary.

Question: are Philip and David true cofounders?

Resources: expertise

Commitment: five hours a week of project work which will be paid + 10% financing

Risk: 10% of the financing to start the business – about 2.000 each

The risk element being very low – limited to 2.000 in cash spend, the situation of Philip and David is not much different from independent contractors. The financial investment could be considered a marketing payment for acquiring projects. If they join the business later – once they will be fully paid from the time of joining – their situation will be more similar to employees. Again, Marianne can decide to give them equity to increase their motivation, but Philip's and David's willingness to take risk is not enough to qualify as true cofounders. Marianne's exposure – with over 16.000 cash investment and full-time (potentially unpaid) work for six months, which is the expected time needed to develop the business to pay her a salary – is incomparably higher.

You can still decide to give your equity away ⌐
of course. The principle that risk equals reward ⌐
to work with, as later on if other equity holders
exposure, their decisions about the business m
with the cofounder(s).

> ## "Where d'you wanna go?
> ## How much you wanna risk?"
>
> *Something just Like This* - The Chainsmokers & Coldplay

Understanding Yourself And Your Cofounders

In the beginning, you might feel the strong urge to move ahead. You are aware of all the things that need to be done and might feel the burning platform, not wanting to miss any opportunities and just run with it.

In this stage, it is very common to assume that your vision, motivation, drivers, ambition and ways of working are aligned or you will figure it out later. Assumption being one of the frequent disaster causes, most cofounders could not be more wrong.

The opportunity here is a big one. And the consequences to miss it are equally big – in the negative sense. It is not about being the same, it is about being aware of the existing differences before you commit to each other. As with so many things in life, prevention is better than correction. The advantage of having the talk with your potential cofounders before you 'tie the knot' is that it allows you to identify the differences and evaluate whether you can work with them. Or whether they are so fundamental that you prefer not to.

..ng the constraints, limited resources and very often also the
to move fast (do you remember Kim's case study?) we will focus
on the minimum essential requirements that you really do need to
understand about your prospective cofounders before you move to
the next steps.

Drivers and motivation

Based on one of the most detailed researches on startup founders
done by Professor Noam Wasserman[8] there are two main drivers
influencing how entrepreneurs make decisions with respect to
their companies. Remembering that entrepreneurship is a more
challenging and risky choice than pursuing more traditional career
tracks, he found out that entrepreneurs are either driven by profit
or control. And according to his research it is not a good strategy to
focus on both. Constantly balancing these two objectives leads, more
often than not, to not achieving either. After having worked with
many inspirational cofounding teams I also feel the need to add one
additional driver: the impact driver. This is because after reaching the
black numbers and being able to pay themselves salaries, the main
driver for some entrepreneurs is to have an impact. Unlike profit and
control, impact might not have a universal definition and depends a
lot on the individual values.

What does that mean in practice? Your main driver – and the one of
your cofounders – is going to be one of the main influencers on the
future strategic decisions of your business. Let's take an example of
the growth of your business: you can choose organic growth (growing
from investing the cash that the business generates) versus external
financing (getting an external investor). If you are profit driven, you
might want to consider getting external financing on board earlier
rather than later – to grow faster. If you are control driven, you will

---

8   Wasserman, N. (2012). The Founder's Dilemmas, p. 32 onwards. Princeton & Oxford,
USA: Princeton University Press

do the opposite: you will look for ways how to bootstrap
longest possible time and then grow organically in order not
up equity in your company to external investors. If you are impact
driven you will evaluate the external investor fit with the values and
vision of the business as the first step before deciding whether getting
her on board is going to add to the impact. If it means faster growth
but deviating from the original vision, the decision might be no. If
it means faster growth *and* increasing the impact, the decision might
be yes. If it means increasing impact but slower growth, the decision
might still be yes. The impact on the control of the company or the
profit is for you secondary.

> "It's okay to spend a lot of
> time arguing about which
> route to take to San Francisco
> when everyone wants to end
> up there, but a lot of time gets
> wasted in such arguments if
> one person wants to go to San
> Francisco and another secretly
> wants to go to San Diego."
>
> Steve Jobs

Gabriel and Lena opened an innovative barber studio together. They are equal partners. While Lena is control driven, Gabriel is profit driven. They did not talk about it at the beginning of their business partnership. After a very successful first 12 months they received an offer from an external investor who would like to join and provide financing for an ambitious growth plan: to open three new studios in the next six months. Gabriel is very excited and wants to move on with the investor's offer, realising that it will enable them to grow much faster. Lena on the other hand prefers to keep the full control of the business between the two of them and grow slower, using the cash flow that the first studio generates. Lena's goal is similar: to open three new studios but in the next 24 months. This decision needs to have both partners on board. Gabriel feels very frustrated that Lena is blocking the progress of the business. Lena does not understand why Gabriel would even consider the offer. The misunderstanding and resentment between the two founders is negatively impacting their business, as the employees start feeling the tension.

Had they had the discussion at the beginning of their partnership, they would have both known if they wanted to go to the same destination. It is not all doomed now, however with the emotions being high and the desired direction so different, they have the difficult task to decide whether they want under these circumstances to continue together or separate. And depending how reasonable and sensible they both are, they will either find a way or the whole business concept is, despite the initial commercial success, under threat.

Core Values and Beliefs

Our core values are something we might not necessarily have on the top of our mind all the time. They do however – consciously or unconsciously – influence every decision that we make in our lives and business and are the basis of our beliefs.

One of the most accurate definitions I came across defines core values as 'the fundamental beliefs of a person or organisation. These guiding principles dictate behaviour and can help people understand the difference between right and wrong. Core values also help companies to determine if they are on the right path and fulfilling their goals by creating an unwavering guide.'[9] Core values typically guide our internal conduct as well as relationship with the external world.[10]

Any decision that is ahead of you – and there will be many – is much easier and quicker if you do not have to draw the map for each step of the way. Because if your cofounding team spends the time to draw the map before you start travelling together you can always take it out of your pocket and use it whenever needed. This will help you to move clearer and faster.

The personal core values of the cofounding team will have a direct influence on creating your business core values. It is very important before you decide to start a business partnership to understand each other's core values because they will have an influence on every decision you will make on the way – from which clients you want to work with to who you would consider hiring as an employee.

In the psychological literature, values and beliefs are distinguished and we could have a long discussion on what is the cause and what is the effect. For the pragmatic purposes of what you want and need to

---

9   Y. (2017, July 10). Examples of Core Values. Retrieved July 21, 2017, from http://examples. yourdictionary.com/examples-of-core-values.html

10   Retrieved July 21, 2017, from http://www.businessdictionary.com/definition/core-values. html

know about your cofounders we will leave the theory aside and focus on what is relevant for the business.

Some of the personal core values that you might want to use as a starting point for the discussion are:

- Dependability
- Diligence
- Truthfulness
- Perseverance
- Reliability
- Loyalty
- Commitment
- Open-mindedness
- Consistency
- Efficiency
- Innovation

- Creativity
- Good humour
- Compassion
- Spirit of adventure
- Motivation
- Positivity
- Optimism
- Passion
- Respect
- Courage
- Service to others

This list is an indicative example and you need to make sure that whichever core values are dear to you, and you want to reflect in the business, are considered and discussed with your future potential cofounders.

While some people are very aware and conscious about their core values, for others they are more under the surface. It is quite difficult for anyone to buy into company core values if they are not clear about their personal values. To avoid confusion, a useful (not only for business) and very much recommended task is for everyone from your prospective team to confirm (or find out) what their personal values are before being able to confirm their alignment with the business.

 You can find as your starting point helpful websites, tools and templates overview in the resource section on cofounding.info

 Martin and Kathrin decide to start a branding agency together. After the first few clients the business starts to grow very fast. One of their potentially biggest projects on the horizon is for a big pharmaceutical company. Securing this project would ensure stable cash flow for the business for the next 18 months and enable expanding the team with five new employees. Martin wants to move ahead and close the deal. Kathrin, however, is against this step, as for her it is important to not work for tobacco and pharmaceutical companies – so much so that she is refusing to continue the business partnership. Without Kathrin, Martin cannot do the deal alone. As he sees the potential of keeping working together, he decides to let the deal go. They both realise that they need to talk more in detail about their core values to agree on which clients they want to consider in the future. Just in time, this disagreement does not damage their business relationship and they are able to continue.

 Anna and Nicole open a physiotherapy practice. Both having their own clients as they start, they agree to combine forces and grow the practice by hiring two extra employees. One of the candidates is a single mother of a young child. While Anna would like to hire her because of her outstanding qualifications, Nicole is hesitating. Anna cannot believe that the private situation of the candidate could be discouraging Nicole to consider the best candidate they have. In her world, it is an absolute no go and she is shocked by what she perceives as her business partner's discriminatory view. As they are both equal partners, they encounter quite early in the partnership a deadlock situation which they are not able to resolve, and decide not to continue with the partnership. The start of the partnership – and its dissolution – would have probably not happened had they discussed their core values before entering the partnership.

Mission and vision

Your vision/purpose/why for the business is the big picture that does directly determine some of the decisions you might face as a team sooner rather than later. It is not a theoretical concept that you might postpone until there is more time or you need to write the first press release! It is not a bunch of fluffy words that you will figure out later to the vision/mission section for your website or annual report. Especially when coming from a corporate environment, you might be sceptical and tend to dismiss spending your valuable time on such topics. However, it is the red thread that should be weaved into your business plan, team, employees, company culture, customers, and all that you do. You want to be clear that everyone on your cofounding team buys into it and is willing to use it as a compass for the future decisions that you as a team will need to make.

Life situation and context

Another aspect you want to make sure you understand about each of your cofounders is understanding where the future business will be in the context of the cofounder's life. I am not saying that you need to know every detail about your cofounder's private life. I am saying you want to understand their context to the extent that it may influence the business that you are planning together.

Remember:

- Just because you work in a certain way, it does not mean everyone else does.

- Trust and openness about potential issues is one of the basic elements of partnership.

Work-life balance

We are different in many things. For you, your life might be a true reflection of work hard, play hard. And your vitality and energy levels make it possible to work 16 hours a day, play for four and four hours of sleep being more than enough. Please do not assume that this is how everyone else lives. Your brother-in-law, with whom you are discussing opening a trading company, wants to do it so that he will have more time with his children and plans to work a maximum eight hours a day with a flexible schedule so he can pick up the kids from school. If you know that and are consciously saying yes to it, it will work. If you did not, sooner or later you will become annoyed with him showing up and leaving unexpectedly and you might get the feeling that he is not contributing to the business as much as you do. And he will get annoyed with your tempo which, from his perspective, is very workaholic-like and with your disrespect for his private family time.

Exit plans

The reasons entrepreneurs start their own business are different. Next to the profit, control or impact drivers, what also differs is the time horizon they plan to be involved in the business and how they would like to exit. They do not have to be the same but being aware of the time horizon and preferred exit is a necessary part of the business plan. If your cofounder's main motivation to join the business is to retire in three years, and yours is to build a worldwide empire, the strategy for the same business will be very different. The type of clients, projects, planning and financing are all decisions that depend on the time horizon that you plan to be involved in with the business. Unless you have an alignment in your team – or at the minimum an understanding of the different expectations – you might end up in endless discussions on the topic.

 Dominik, Robert and Roger start an architectonic studio. Dominik (55), Robert (41) and Roger (37) were working together before and found a market niche in which all three of them are specialists. For Dominik, the most important objective is to enjoy freedom to decide on his own projects and be able to retire in the next five years. For Robert and Roger the main objective is to grow the company. Their different objectives are not a show stopper, but it is important that they talk about it, as for Dominik, the preferred option would be to sell the company in the next five years if an opportunity arises. As long as they are aware of and communicate transparently about the difference, they can successfully navigate as a team towards an exit strategy for Dominik while achieving the goals for Robert and Roger.

Financial requirements

Especially in the beginning investment phase, you need to be aware of your cofounders' financial situation. Whether it is to be able to calculate how long you can bootstrap, or if you can internally raise the capital needed for your business growth, or to know if the cofounders' commitment is realistic. Again, it is not about all cofounders having the same situation, but about the awareness if there are significant differences. If one of you is ready to invest over the next three years in growing the business without expectation of financial rewards and one of you needs to ensure income coming in after six months, you need to take it into consideration.

A few decisions that may be heavily influenced by this are, for example: whether to take on a financial liability within the company; distributing versus reinvesting profits; or whether to include cofounder salaries in your cash flow forecast.

Health

Health is another private life category that should remain private unless it could interfere with the planned commitments. The basic trust and respect of future business partners dictate disclosure to the team of any potential health issues that could interfere with the business. Again, existence of them is not necessarily a deal breaker, but awareness allows for integration and planning. Examples of points that should be raised, in the initial stages, are expected or planned surgery, expected or planned pregnancy, or recovery from illness or accident that requires regular health practitioner visits or less than a full-time work schedule. The commitment to the business is one aspect, another one being what type of insurance and coverage for the cofounders you want to include and what are the risks you need to manage (contingency planning for example).

Risk tolerance

Entrepreneurship is a risky path. The range of possible options is between being wildly successful and selling your company in a few years to becoming bankrupt in a few months. And anything in between. And the risk tolerance with which each of your potential cofounders operates will again impact how they will decide. Whether it is the decision to invest (more of) your own capital into the business or take on external liabilities (bank loan). It is one of the potential benefits of having the team to have different levels of risk tolerance and therefore different opinions. You just want to know about the differences, and how they might influence the future decisions of your team, upfront.

Family situation

The personal context of our lives is another factor not to be ignored. Your cofounders can be anywhere between single fully dedicated workaholics to parents of three young children who also need to take care of their own ageing relatives. And the family situation does not influence how valuable your selected cofounders could be for the business. It does influence though their possible commitment and availability. The degree of family support for the business might also influence how much motivation and perseverance your cofounders will have.

Some of the war stories I came across also included – in conflict situations – the spouses of the cofounders influencing the cofounders in ways which were not exactly constructive for finding a solution. Life partner choice is absolutely a private area, but having at a minimum an understanding of your prospective cofounder's situation is definitely a recommended part of due diligence.

Another question you might want to discuss is if you or any of your cofounders expect to involve their family members in the business in the future.

What Happens If?

Life in general has a good sense of humour. If you are the analytical future-thinking type, it might have happened to you that you spent time thinking about X possible scenarios for a situation and that what happened was the X+1 scenario you did not include in your list of options. This situation is relatively common and frequent especially in the dynamic early stage of business environment. The recommended approach very often is to test, learn, adjust, succeed – in the spirit of the lean startup. This means that your business strategy, product, service, planned next steps, marketing strategy – pretty much almost every element of your business – can and most likely will change.

And that is fine. It is neither wise nor realistically possible to be too rigid in the beginning. And it is not possible to foresee every scenario. Simulating some of them is however a good way to learn more about your cofounders, how your potential future team decides and also test the alignment of your team.

Scenario Simulation Exercise

Get your team together, reserve some time and dive into some of the possible scenarios that can happen – and test how your team would decide. The process is as valuable as the outcome. Your team can get a lot of value from this exercise: observe *how* the discussion is made. Who talks most? Who is a good listener (verbal and nonverbal?)? Did you feel heard? Who summarised? Who facilitated? Who was the timekeeper? Who was the voice of the customer? How was a decision reached? By majority voting (was that rule agreed upfront?) Or otherwise? If one would observe from the outside, what would a witness say about your discussion and decision? What were the learnings from that? What should you all:

1. Keep doing.

2. Start doing.

3. Stop doing in future discussions?

Finance what ifs

Under which conditions would you consider getting an external investor, loan or how do you foresee dealing with cash flow issues if they occur? What is each cofounder's maximum time they can invest without receiving money from the business? Would the cofounders be willing to provide a personal loan to the business if needed? What is their risk tolerance?

Employees what ifs

When do you foresee hiring employees? Who would you consider? Hiring family members, yes or no? Is it OK to have intimate relationships with employees? What will you do if that happens?

Personal what ifs

What will happen in case of any cofounder having an accident or serious health issues? Loss of motivation or interest? If any of the cofounders would receive an attractive offer? If any of the cofounders have serious personal crises? Would you as a team consider hiring a cofounder family member? What happens if a cofounder develops an intimate private relationship within the business?

Any red flags?

You might have already noticed that the process to select and form the cofounding team is equally as important as the outcome. It will not only help you to select the right cofounders, but it will also help you to identify if there are significant differences and to resolve them – upfront. Or alternatively you identify significant differences and you will not be able to resolve them, in which case you do not move forward. As frustrating as it is, it is better to split before you start if your potential cofounders are not the right fit.

The Essential Ingredients Of Successful Partnerships

Not being exclusive for the success of business partnerships, nor being an exclusive list, the main essential ingredients for any successful and sustainable partnerships are:

- Open and transparent communication

- Trust

- Respect

And it is important that these ingredients are present in the whole team. If you have a good communication with your other two cofounders for example, but they cannot communicate openly between each other, your team will not be functioning properly. The chain is always as strong as its weakest part. So in evaluating if your team has the essential ingredients to function, especially if some of the cofounders have longer existing relationships than others, you need to examine the whole team but also across the individual cofounders' relationships.

Open and transparent communication

One of the most frequent and most overlooked warning flags that you might have experienced is not feeling comfortable to discuss some of the topics that we talked about in the previous sections with your cofounders. If that is so, have a look at what is causing the discomfort. It can be you – perhaps not wanting to hear a clear answer that you know could be a show stopper while you so badly want to move ahead. Or it can be that you do not have a good communication culture within the team. In any case, if you do not feel comfortable to openly communicate with your future business partners, you do not want to continue. Whatever the reason is, it will come and bite you later.

Trust

Whether it is to speak about what are the cofounders' expectations from joining the business or about the future commitment to the business, it requires a basic level of trust. And you do need to have a basic level of trust with your cofounders. Later, when we speak about the roles and responsibilities of the team or the milestones (to which you might perhaps also link the equity allocation), you will still need to have basic project management good practices – from measuring to evaluating your cofounders' team performance. But you want to have them within a trusting environment. And this is true not only in the relationship between you and the other cofounders but also in the relationship between the other cofounders. This is typically an overlooked point when you bring together cofounders that you know but they do not know each other yet. If at any point during the discussion you feel that the level of trust – in the team or with any of the cofounders – is not optimal, address it, and if not sufficient, take the steps needed to build it. You need to create a safe environment where the cofounders feel free to express (possibly dissenting) opinions. According to Google's two-year-long study where they observed over 180 Google teams, looking for the secret ingredient of high-performing teams, psychological safety – an environment 'in which everyone is safe to take risks, voice their opinions, and ask judgment-free questions' – was one of the key five characteristics.[11]

Respect

One of the main benefits of having a team as opposed to going solo is the diversity of backgrounds, opinions and preferences, and to be able to benefit from it you need to be able to respect each other's opinions and differences in the team. Doing some of the exercises of this chapter was a great testing ground of your team and ability to respect each other's opinions. Respect does not mean that you need to agree; respect means that you give each cofounder a space to share their opinion and give it careful consideration as a team. Similarly to the previous ingredients, being open communication and trust, if you have doubts whether your team has the level of respect required for the team to work successfully in the future, investigate and correct first.

Creating the alter ego

This is my favourite and the credit for formulating this one goes to Paco Savio of the Balboa team, a very interesting, innovative and successful fitness concept born in Zurich. When asked how they

---

11 Schneider, M. (2017, July 19). Google Spent 2 Years Studying 180 Teams. The Most Successful Ones Shared These 5 Traits. Retrieved July 26, 2017, from https://www.inc.com/michael-schneider/google-thought-they-knew-how-to-create-the-perfect.html?cid=cp01002fastco

managed in their very diverse cofounder team to make it work, Paco pointed out an obvious but very often overlooked aspect. That in any relationship between people who decide to create something together, you need to put the individual egos aside, throw them into a big melting pot and create an alter ego of whatever it is you are creating together. And that becomes more important than your individual ego – whether you are right or wrong. This corresponds to the psychological concept of transpersonal will: a higher goal which is greater, or transcends, the individual goal.[12] This is an element that comes over time, as you start working together. Just do not forget to add it to the existing base of open communication, trust and respect, and nurture all of them, all the time.

Do not ignore any red flags now. It is much more difficult to resolve conflicts in the heat of the business on the way, when the business pressure, investment and emotions can be already mixing in, than to do it before being committed together.

Just because you are certain does not mean you are right. Do test your assumptions and understanding of your cofounders' context. Does your future dream team have the open communication, trust and respect to be able to work together? Remember that you are creating the team to help you realise your dreams, not your nightmares. And you are responsible to be honest with yourself and the other cofounders to give it the best shot you can.

Please pay attention:

- If you do not feel right about something it most probably is not right.

- Do not ignore any red flags and move ahead without resolving them.

- Wishful thinking seldom resolves significant differences.

---

12 For more information you can check: *The Act of Will* by Roberto Assagioli

Team Building Exercise

 Open communication, trust and respect are the essential ingredients of a successful partnership and they are not automatic.

Helpful exercises to create or deepen these aspects that you can do are:

1. Team building exercise based on the Lassalle Institute Model:[13]

   a) Uniqueness: everybody in the founding team is unique in her way of being and skills – ask every cofounder what is her unique selling point which she brings to the team.

   b) Diversity: we are all different, with different skills and development areas. How will we make sure as a team that we value the diversity in everyday operations?

   c) Union: despite our differences, what glues us together? What is our shared vision? What unites us? What is the dream we share?

2. 'Cocktail party' exercise: this exercise is good for starting teams and also repeated regularly. Play music in the background and get real – stand up, walk about with a drink, pair up and tell each other (no answering allowed) just listening and acknowledging nonverbally:

   a) I like working with you because…

   b) I admire in you that you…

   c) I would love to learn from you…

---

13 Lassalle-Institut Zen Ethik Leadership. (n.d.). Retrieved July 28, 2017, from https://www. lassalle-institut.info/ or directly: Communio Institut fur Furhrungskunst. (n.d.). Retrieved July 28, 2017, from http://www.communio-fuehrungskunst.de/de/pers_spirit/methoden/lassalle.php

d) The last time you made me really angry was when…

e) The thing I always wanted to tell you is…

f) What I wish for the most from you is…

g) An attitude/behaviour you really have to stop is…

After that, no discussions are allowed – have a total silence for 10 minutes. The next five minutes use for everyone feeling into what was just said. For another five minutes, everyone takes personal notes. After that, share with the team. No discussion allowed. Only clarification questions.

Concluding Remarks

Important to realise is that many of the aspects mentioned in this chapter are formed very early in life – core values, beliefs, capacity to trust – and are relatively stable throughout our lives. There are varying opinions on how much we can change them with personal development efforts. That aside, it is a good assumption to take what you learnt at face value and not to assume that you, the business, team dynamics or anything else in the future cooperation will change the cofounder. So work with what you have. And based on that decide whether you want to move to the next step or not.

If you have the resources, it is very helpful for this step to have a session with an external facilitator so everyone can concentrate on learning about the other cofounders and the team dynamics.

Checklist

- Each cofounder has passed the cofounders test – by bringing the required resources, commitment and taking risk.

- I understand my own and each cofounders' main drivers (profit, control, impact).

- I understand my own and each cofounders' core values.

- I understand my own and each cofounders' context.

- We did the scenario exercise with the team.

- We have the essential ingredients within the team (open communication, trust, respect).

CHAPTER 4:

DATING TIMES

04 Dating times

- Working styles
- Personality differences
- Try before you buy

In this chapter you will learn:

- Typical development stages of high-performing teams.

- Why it is important to get a feel about your cofounders' personalities.

- What you need to know about your cofounders' working styles.

- Which future scenarios you want to run through with your cofounders.

Dating times are extremely important before you decide to get serious with your potential cofounders, for a few reasons: to confirm what you learnt about your cofounders in the previous step; get to know them better – working styles, personalities, annoying traits; and also to test how the team works together. Because even the best selected individual players might not necessarily be the best team; you need the right mixture, dynamics and the essential ingredients. And testing if you have that will allow you to move through the stages to create the high-performing team faster.

High Performing Teams Development Stages

As Rome was not built in a day, great teams do not start with a high performance from day one. The team development stages model was formulated in the '70s by Dr Bruce Tuckman, an American psychologist. According to this model, all the development stages are necessary and inevitable to get the team to high-performance mode.

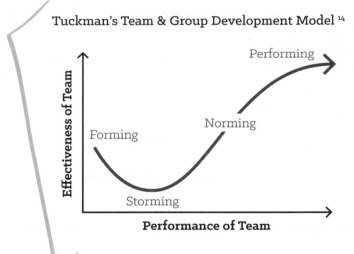

Tuckman's Team & Group Development Model [14]

1. Forming: this stage happens in the beginning as the team meets, gets familiar with what they are going to do together and then agrees on a plan of how to do it. In this stage, the team members tend to behave rather independently and are on their best behaviour – trying

14 Tuckman's Team & Group Development Model: What You Need To Know To Get Your New Group or Team Performing Beautifully! (2017, March 11). Retrieved July 22, 2017, from https://www.thecoachingtoolscompany.com/get-your-team-performing-beautifully-with-this-powerful-group-development-model/

to look good and demonstrating socially desirable behaviour. It is an orientation stage – with the task and with each other. The most effective leadership style for this stage is directive.

2. Storming: in this stage, the team members begin to form opinions about the other team members. They are testing the boundaries and looking to establish their own position within the team. Conflicts, tension, arguments and power struggles can occur during this stage. Depending on the maturity, tolerance and ability to compromise of the team members, this stage will either make the team stronger or can cause the team to break up. The most effective leadership style for this stage is coaching.

3. Norming: 'resolved disagreements and personality clashes result in greater intimacy and a spirit of co-operation emerges'.[15] The common goal, or alter ego, of the project replaces the individual identities, with toleration of the now known whims and fancies of the other team members. Roles and responsibilities become clear and accepted. Respect for each other enables the team to move to the next stage. The most effective leadership style for this stage is facilitating and empowering.

4. Performing: in this stage, the team is focused on achieving common goals. The team members are autonomous, empowered and feel competent to focus on the task in a trusting environment. They have learned how to communicate and are comfortable with dissenting opinions; they face challenges, find solutions and deliver results. The most effective leadership style for this stage is supporting and delegating.

---

15 Raynolds, J. & Chatfield, R. (2007). Leadership the Outward Bound way: becoming a better leader in the workplace, in the wilderness, and in your community. Seattle: Mountaineers Books

> **"Finding good players is easy, getting them to play together as a team is another story."**
>
> Casey Stangel

Any change in the team – be it a team member joining or leaving or a change in leadership – might require the team to go back to some of the previous stages. Even without a change in the members or leadership, the team might from time to time reiterate the different phases as it is continuously evolving. An example might be when a new task or skill is required, a new project or client is acquired or the focus of the business changes.

Understanding these stages can help you to move the team to the desired performing stage as effectively and efficiently as possible, maximising the learnings from the previous stages and adjusting the leadership style depending on which stage the team is going through.

Working Style And Personalities

What do you ideally want to know about your future business partners when it comes to their working style? And what should they know about yours? The more knowledge you have, the faster you are able to move and navigate the team through the development stages and later on utilise this knowledge in organising and managing the team – from allocation of roles and responsibilities to daily operations.

> **"Most important about styles is not the similarities or differences but how you manage to capitalise on them."**
>
> David Gage

And having fun along the road!

Goals and priorities

For some cofounders, a priority in having their own business is to have a flexible working schedule. For others, it is the prestige of being an entrepreneur. Some of them are complementary, some level each other out and some are competing. And most of them can be used to maximise your team performance if you know them upfront. This is also important to understand before you decide on your team roles, responsibilities and how you work together.

There is a famous story of having the cake and eating it. There are two purchasing teams from different companies and they both have a task to secure the one and only available supply of one ton of oranges. One company needs it to develop a drug to prevent small babies' diarrhoea which could be deadly and there is a current outbreak. The other company needs it to produce a cancer medication for their very promising last stage of a clinical trial; without securing the supplies the trial results will not be possible to use, delaying the potential cure by months. Both have very urgent reasons, unlimited budget authorisation and a very strong case why their company should be the one to get the supply. After hours of heated bidding discussion with the seller, a team member of one of the buyers asks the other one what exactly they need. It turns out that one company needs the orange peels, while the other one needs the fresh juice. While this may be an extreme example and a beautiful story with a happy ending, the lesson here is that understanding the exact needs can help us find better win-win set-ups.

We will come back to this point when discussing the equity ownership, as the priority for some of your cofounders can be control, while for the others it can be the profit potential. And understanding the main underlying motivation will help you to structure your team better.

Strengths and development opportunities

To get the maximum out of the team you do want to know each cofounder's strengths and development opportunities. In the beginning, and in small teams, it is possible that you will need to have flexibility between the roles and sometimes the different cofounders will need to cover for each other. Knowing their respective strengths and development opportunities enables the team leader to assign the tasks to the best possible candidate. If you have a big picture strategist as one of the cofounders who really, but really, is not good with details, you probably do not want this person to evaluate and conclude insurance for your business and ask her to read through all the fine print, compare different offers and decide on the best coverage. Similarly, you do not want the absolutely brilliant engineer who is a little bit shy and awkward in social situations to be responsible for networking events or pitches to the investors.

Annoying traits

Be honest. Everyone has them. You, me, your previous boss, the love of your life, your kids and your future cofounder. If you get a block on this one, ask what would you change about yourself if you could? Is it not being able to see the big picture when you get stressed? Is it the inability to prioritise? Is it coming up with last-minute changes after the final decision has been made and agreed? Is it interrupting others while they speak? Is it showing up always a few minutes late for meetings? Some of the annoying traits we have become more prevalent in high-pressure stress situations. Check for regular behaviour and for stress behaviour patterns. And realise that some characteristics can have two sides of the coin – below is a beautiful example from DISC, a personality characteristics tool, of before and after partnership perspectives.

DISC BEFORE AND AFTER PARTNERSHIP PERSPECTIVES [16]

DISC dimension	Before, we see our partner's strengths as:	After, we see our partner's limitations as:
D	Courageous Efficient Competitive Determined	Reckless Workaholic Overly aggressive Stubborn
I	Enthusiastic Optimistic Persuasive Spontaneous	Excitable Unrealistic Manipulative Disorganised
S	Steadfast Systematic Agreeable Good listener	Resistant to change Slow paced Indecisive Noncommunicative
C	Analytical Serious Orderly Industrious	Critical Unsociable Perfectionist Workaholic

Whenever in the future you find yourself in a difficult moment with any of your cofounders, it does help tremendously to remind each other about the awareness you had in the beginning about it and about the joint commitment to work with it. If we feel we know about potential challenges ahead, we deal with them very often much better than if they come by surprise.

---

16 Gage, D. (2004). The Partnership Charter: How to Start Out Right With Your New Business Partnership (or Fix the One You're In). New York: Basic Books

Perseverance

Perseverance is often cited as one of the most important characteristics of successful entrepreneurs, so you might want to check in your team how much of it you have – both individually and combined. Some of the useful questions to ask are: What would make you quit trying? What do you need to keep going? How much perseverance did you demonstrate in the past in your life?

No Go's

It is also very useful to know – upfront – what are your and your cofounders' absolute No Go's. It could be a style of communication that someone finds very disturbing – for example, authoritarian or agitated. It could be a mode of communication – for example, discussing sensitive issues by email rather than in person. Or it could be violation of the core values – examples being lying, manipulating or belittling.

How you get stuff done

There are many roads that lead to Rome. While you might be the perfectly organised type that plans way ahead of time, builds in sufficient time buffers and whose desk is always clean, your chosen cofounder might be finishing work five minutes before a deadline, having issues prioritising tasks and having chaotic paperwork that only she understands. It is not necessarily the point to create an internal hit parade and evaluate which is better, it is to understand that you do work differently and being able to respect each other's way to achieve the results.

Interests

What are the things each of you absolutely love and hate doing? This conversation is invaluable input for constructive allocation of your team roles and responsibilities. It can happen that your cofounder has a finance and accounting background and she absolutely hates accounting and under no circumstances wants to be involved with it. She is, however, fine to take care of it for the first six months until the business has sufficient cash flow to outsource this.

Preferred way of working

For some teams I worked with, having fun on the go was one of the core principles they defined for working together. For some it can be prioritising efficiency and speed. Someone may need to have a feeling of connection with the partner before they can move on to discuss business issues. Someone thinks better by walking and the other just should not be talked to without having had her morning coffee first. Whatever it is, it might not always be possible to accommodate, but knowing that about each other can, over time, make a lot of difference on how much you will enjoy working together as a team – directly influencing the chances to last and perform.

Personality Tools

Depending on your team seniority and self-awareness, you might have been able to get a good picture of the working style and the main strengths and weaknesses of each cofounder and decide on the basic rules for your cofounding team by discussion only.

Some of the used and useful personality typologies and tools include:

DISC: focusing on behavioural traits – the assessment evaluates dominance (D), influence (I), steadiness (S) and compliance (C). The initial purpose of the assessment is focused on increasing the individual's self-knowledge and awareness and to determine their leadership style as it links different leadership styles to each personality type. It is especially effective for improving communication and strengthening teamwork.

DISC personality segments

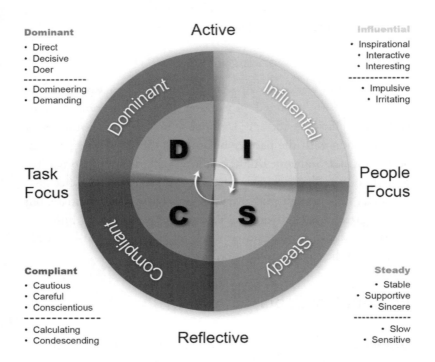

Dominant
- Direct
- Decisive
- Doer

- Domineering
- Demanding

Active

Influential
- Inspirational
- Interactive
- Interesting

- Impulsive
- Irritating

Task Focus

People Focus

Compliant
- Cautious
- Careful
- Conscientious

- Calculating
- Condescending

Reflective

Steady
- Stable
- Supportive
- Sincere

- Slow
- Sensitive

MBTI: the Myers Briggs typology based on the four dichotomies specified in Jung's theory is one of the most often used personality tests. It translates the different character traits in understandable categories on where we prefer to focus (Extraversion or Introversion), how we process information (Sensing or Intuition), how we make decisions (Thinking or Feeling) and how we deal with the outside world (Judging or Perceiving). Different combinations of these attributes create the basic 16 personality types. Although being frequently used and widely spread, the MBTI model is also known for relatively poor validity (not measuring what it says it measures) and poor reliability (giving different results to the same person on different occasions or in different life phases) and in the expert psychologist circles is considered very old-fashioned and generally unreliable.

Big Five personality traits: this theory works with words association in common language and based on that evaluates five dimensions commonly used to describe human personality (openness to experience, conscientiousness, extraversion, agreeableness and neuroticism). It is less practically applicable and prone to gender and cultural differences and is known for its limited scope – not explaining all of human personality.

Gallup StrengthsFinder: the underlying theory being that knowing individual strengths enables them to focus on the strengths instead of weaknesses. The Gallup Strengths catalogue was developed based on empirical experience by distilling 'talent theme' patterns that describe the range of human uniqueness.

Leadership circle profile: is a '360 degree competency assessment that simultaneously provides focused competency feedback while revealing the underlying assumptions and thinking that are causing a leader's pattern of strengths and limitations.'[17] This assessment not only tells you the what, but also the why. It distinguishes two domains of leadership: creative competencies (how you achieve results) and reactive tendencies (emphasising caution and self-limiting styles).

As useful as these tools are in getting to know more about each other, there is no commonly agreed definition of personality and how to measure it even amongst psychologists. Every theory, model and measurement should be taken as approximation because a map is just a map and not the territory. Even the best personality tests show very low validity when being used in forecasting job performance. So take them and use them as a starting point, not a conclusive judgment.

---

17 Leadership Circle Profile™ (n.d.) Retrieved July 22, 2017, from https://leadershipcircle.com/assessment-tools/profile/

You can find as your starting point some of the available tools overview in the resource section on cofounding.info.

Although they have different pros and cons and level of detail, choosing any one of them will give you a good start. Ask all your cofounders to complete and share with the team their results for the assessment of your choice. And have the discussion afterwards – did you identify any red flags? How do you need to structure your team working together to maximise the value of each member? Is anyone on your team an introvert who is unlikely to share their opinion in the group? How do you address it in your joint decision making? Is anyone in your team conflict averse? If so how do you make sure that they do speak up when appropriate and not hide disagreement until explosion point? Does anyone have focus challenges? How can the team help?

The questions you want to discuss will depend on what came up for you and your cofounders, the points above are just examples. It is not about the differences but about being aware of them, mitigating the potential weaknesses and maximising the strengths.

There are many good and validated methodologies on team and project performance; for further reference you might want to explore the spiral dynamics or the AQAL model of Ken Wilbrer.

Try Before You Buy

As much as you can learn about your cofounders from the previous exercise, if there is a chance that you can test it in practice before getting serious, use it! Whether it is working together on a business plan, assigning minor tasks and seeing how they get executed, observing the dynamics between the individual cofounders, use all that you can to learn as much as you can. And be sharp. If people show you who they are, believe them. As with dating, in the initial 'rose-tinted glasses' phase we might have the tendency to overlook what we do not want to see because it does not fit our picture. This is – in both business and private partnerships – not the smartest strategy.

You might even consider to agree on a 'cofounder probation period' – a specified time and task when you decided to work together to test the waters. What is extremely important in this time is to define exactly for everyone involved the framework for the cooperation, including:

- For how long you intend to do it.

- What are the specific tasks and expectations from each party?

- If the cooperation continues after, how it will be structured.

- If the cooperation does not continue after, is there any compensation due to anyone, and if yes, what is the compensation?

- Ownership allocation to any intellectual property, know-how or client relationship that will be developed during this period.

Preferably you would want to summarise this agreement as a Memorandum of Understanding between the parties in writing.

Special attention to this point is recommended for cofounding teams with previous social relationship (friends, family, ex-colleagues). Do also speak about whether and how you are able to compartmentalise your relationship. Think about what you will do if things turn sour (back to the scenarios). Create a disaster plan for the worst case scenarios (kind of a pre-nuptial agreement if you are getting responsibly married) and above all do force these sensitive discussions if you have to. Because if you are not able/willing to do it at the beginning, there is a high chance that later will be even more difficult.

Checklist

- I understand the working styles – including goals, priorities, strengths and weaknesses, no go's, annoying traits and preferred way of working – about my cofounders.

- The cofounders understand this about each other.

CHAPTER 5:

GETTING SERIOUS

05 **Get serious**

- O Roles and reponsibilities
- O Relationships
- O Conversations to have

Now you have confirmed that partnership is right for you, know what you are looking for, preselected potential cofounders and dated with them, it is time to get serious. Step 5 is about:

- Important considerations for allocating the roles and responsibilities in your cofounding team.

- Using the RACI tool to verify your allocation.

- Allocation of titles.

- Which conversations do you need to have as a cofounding team.

Roles And Responsibilities

Why do you want to define these? I know, in the beginning when you are starting, you do expect and need some level of flexibility of your team as your business strategy and model can still go through a few changes before it stabilises.

You need to decide what is the right level of detail or specificity that fits your business and your team. But defining the roles and responsibilities is very important for several reasons. You do not want everyone to be doing everything. It is counterproductive. You also want to make sure that all that needs to be done will get done. And finally, you do need to have clarity and understanding on the individual cofounders' expectations and criteria for evaluating their performance.

Roles

Build on the strengths and preferences

A good start is to think about roles and responsibilities in your team from the strengths and weaknesses of your cofounders, and as much as possible to match the role with what your cofounders love doing. That way you can use each cofounder for what they are best at and most motivated. This, however, needs to fit the use of the resources that you identified that the cofounder will bring. If you invited someone on your team because of his IT skills and the idea is that he will develop the first working prototype, his ambition to be the CFO might not be fitting your business plan.

 Exercise: for testing your team roles allocation, you can use the team dynamics based on Tetra Map ® Model: 4 elements in a team and project

Personality overview based on TetraMap ® model

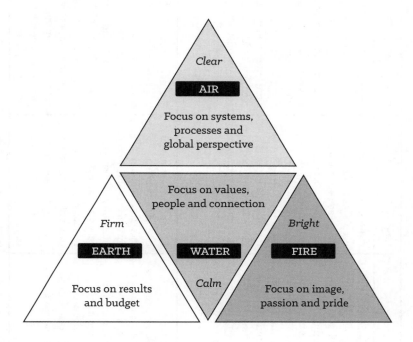

An overview of the type's qualities and how to communicate with them, as well as helpful guidance to identify them is in the table overleaf.

	Earth	Air	Water	Fire
Positive qualities	**Firm**, stable, patient, focus on results, security and budget oriented, attention to detail, trustworthy, tradition and regulation/policy focused, facts oriented, perfectionism, there when one needs her, only speaks if she has something to say.	**Clear**, full of ideas, freedom oriented, conceptual, sees overall picture/ connects the dots, thinks in processes and value chains, system and global thinker, strategic, future trends, very fast thinker, not afraid of being wrong: the truth/best possible option is more important than ego.	**Calm**, focused on values, people, relationships and the greater good, building connections between parties, holding the team together, flexible and soothing in being, striving towards balance and peace, having a good time with another, focuses on contribution.	**Bright**, brave, no fear of confrontation, quick, giving direction, passion, pride, (financial) success oriented, energy, emotional, assertive, forward going, extraverted, traditionally seen as a leader, control and power-oriented, 'I can do it on my own'.
Negative qualities	Rigid/inflexible, difficult to convince, blocked in their action, risk-averse/too cautious, lacking bigger picture/imagination, too secretive, future averse, overregulation, wanting to be right, errors are an attack to her core, too introvert, not speaking up.	Confused, too many ideas, building air castles, missing reality, can't see the wood for the trees, day-dreaming, too fast/impatient, too many mistakes or doesn't care, insecurity regarding own skills (not knowledge), inaction.	Lacking forward energy or profile, avoiding (necessary) conflict, unable to bear tension or insecurity, choosing the easy way out, indecisive, relationships too much over task/ facts, not too interested in due dates, insecure about her own contribution.	Emotionally blackmailing others with tantrums, too dominant and risk affine, smart without being wise, leading for the sake of being the 'Alpha', not connected with (own) deeper feelings or others', not trusting, impatient, judgmental, one solution only, lonely rider.

	Earth	Air	Water	Fire
Key sentences	'Let's look at the risks first!' 'What does that cost and who will do it?' 'What will be our contingency plan?'	'The future is so bright!' 'There is this new Google research on…' 'We could just do it the other way round!'	'We should do it together.' 'We haven't heard Andrea yet…' 'That was an unfair comment!'	'I am there already, where are you?' 'Be brief, be bright, be gone!' 'Time is money!'
Best suited role	**Reality checker:** She will identify what won't work and execute the rest perfectly.	**Visionary:** She inspires, sees trends, the future and the bigger picture.	**Stakeholder Mistress:** She understands and holds all parties in balance.	**Engine and fuel:** Let her passion ignite action and give direction to the team.
Most difficult and fruitful relationship with	Airy colleague	Earthy colleague	Fiery colleague	Watery colleague

	Earth	Air	Water	Fire
Questions to explore this tendency	How important is **security** to you?	How important is **freedom** for you?	How important is being calm and balanced for you?	How important is having **influence** to you?
	What makes you take immediate **action**?	If you look for **new ideas**, what do you do?	How do you **contribute** to the team?	How many **possible** solutions are there to solve a problem?
	What would **freak you out** the most?	What **skills** do qualify you most for this role?	How do you approach **conflict**?	What **emotions** do you feel when looking at your team?
	Who would you be if you didn't know the **facts**?	Who would you be if you couldn't **inspire** others?	Who would you be if you didn't bring **harmony** into a team?	Who would you be if you weren't in the **first** row?
Way to communicate with them	Emphasise the challenge: **Just** do it!	Emphasise her abilities: You have the **skills**, do it!	Emphasise their contribution: I **trust** you can do it!	Emphasise their possibilities: Let's **do** it!

The table above is developed by an organisational psychologist Nicole Menten, exclusively for this book and is inspired by Tetra Map®, aiming by no means at being complete or 'right'. Neither does it claim to display recent academic research. It should rather be seen as a simple tool and possible starting point for role allocation in the cofounding team. And it certainly should not be used to put anyone in one of the boxes for eternity and realise that we all have all the four elements in us and they become pronounced depending on the context.

The practical takeaway for your team role allocation is:

a. Put the 'airy' people at the beginning of the project/founding phase: there you need the visionaries, the ones with ideas, strategic thinking, concepts, idealists and manage their downside being possibly too optimistic with their head in the clouds.

b. Let the 'earthy' people play either consciously the devil's advocate and/or put them on the project later for implementation as their typical strengths are attention to detail, reality check, numbers, structures, processes, benchmarking, and manage their downside being overthinking which could lead to no action, risk averseness and pessimism.

c. Get 'fiery' people to ignite the earthy ones, light their passion, motivate the other to have 'skin in the game', action energy, going forward. Managing the downside being impatience, too quick, prone to errors, too dominant, 'my way or the highway' decision approach.

d. Get 'watery' people, to hold the team together, they are flexible, good with ambiguity, meandering around obstacles, they bring softness and caring, and are able to extinguish the heat of the other three types.

Common traps

Common traps you do not want to fall into include:

Having multiple people for the same role

This is confusing. The more the roles overlap, the more time might get spent on clarifying who is doing what, and why your other cofounder was expecting you to take care of it – because you share it and he thinks you are better at it.

Having too narrowly defined roles

Balance is everything. In the early stages you might need more flexibility; if you define the roles too narrowly you might need to change it very frequently as the business develops.

Having too broadly defined roles

The other side of the coin is that if you define roles too broadly it will not be clear enough what is expected and who is supposed to do what.

Not choosing the leader

Perhaps you have more candidates who want to do the job. Or between your cofounders there is no one who would be capable to do it right. In either scenario it is not a situation that you want to accept for long. Decision making can become very complex and ships without a captain most of the time do not enjoy smooth sailing, nor do they reach their desired destination. If you have more candidates and you have problems either discussing it or choosing, it might indicate communication issues in your team. Or inexperience. If you do not have a leader it clearly is a gap in your cofounding team that you want to close as soon as possible. And yes, as the business grows or goes to the next stage you might need to change the leader. You just do not want to start without one.

Shared roles

Sometimes the tendency to avoid sensitive discussion or feeling egalitarian leads to opting for joint roles (for example CEO). No one says it cannot be you who will be walking on the moon. However, if you want to learn from the experience of countless others before you, and focus on the business, do not do this. These arrangements just do not work – mid and long term. Next to being rather slow (consensus takes time), it leads to confusion of your team and the dislike and distrust of investors.

Responsibilities

Even if you assume that the role is clear enough it is worth the extra little bit of effort to list the main responsibilities of the roles. It is very important for everyone to know what is expected and you also want to have the clarity, in case you need to address lack of performance in the team. The responsibilities which you define for each role will prove to be invaluable guidance if you need to address underperformance in the team or, in the worst case scenario, fire a cofounder for non-performance. Without it you might end up in a very difficult situation evaluating what a non-performance is. As with so many other situations, I wish for you that you never to have to do that. However, history, countless other cofounders' experiences and statistics suggest that it is a possible risk. And having clear roles and responsibilities is making the risk smaller for your whole team.

 Exercise: Use the RACI model to double-check.

During my years of business restructuring we used the RACI model for describing roles and responsibilities. It is a straightforward and simple tool to check if your roles and responsibilities in the cofounding team are done right:

You create a matrix of roles and the main responsibilities. As a next step, you go through the responsibilities and assign for each one:

R: the Responsible: the owner of the responsibility – who is expected to get it done.

A: the Approver: who is expected to approve before the responsibility is effective; this can be together with R or separate.

C: the Consulted: who has information or knowledge to be used for executing the responsibility.

I: the Informed: who should know about how the responsibility is executed.

RACI template

Team members	Roles	
Cofounder 1	R	Responsible: person working on activity
Cofounder 2	A	Accountable: person with decision authority
Cofounder 3	C	Consult: key stakeholder who should be in
Cofounder 4	I	Inform: needs to know about decision or action
Cofounder 5		

Activity	CF1	CF2	CF3	CF4	CF5
Develop business plan	A	R	I	I	C
Confirm business model	I	C	A	R	C
CX testing	I	C	C	A	R
Product market fit strategy	I	AR	I	C	I
Seed financing acquisition	A	C	C	R	I
Prepare incorporation	I	A	R	C	C
Develop cofounder agreement	C	C	C	C	AR
Other …					

Link the activities in the RACI tool to your business plan and project plan for the next actionable period to also double-check that you allocated all activities that need to happen and the team has the resources to execute them.

What is the benefit of doing the exercise? For every responsibility you should always have only one person responsible. Because wisdom and experience tells us that the more people that share the responsibility, the less chance there is that it will be done. And you might want to have more people or the whole team to approve (the A), to give input (the C) or to know about it (the I).

Now you might think this sounds too complex. It will only be as complex as you make it – the level of detail for the responsibilities list. But it is a great tool to help you identify if you either have a gap i.e. no-one is responsible, or overlap i.e. more cofounders are responsible.

 You can find as your starting point the RACI template in the resource section on cofounding.info.

Titles

What do you want to know before you decide on your cofounding team titles?

- Beware of title inflation: it is not uncommon, not only in the startup world, to witness the title inflation. Yesterday's cleaner is today's facility manager. As much as we see this happening everywhere, it is not necessarily a recommendable trend. Yes, it might sound very attractive to have everyone in your team being a C-level (Chief of something). However, this can backfire in two ways. One is not being taken seriously if your team only have C-roles, but no team to manage. The other is, as your business matures, you may need to create a regular organisation structure and reassign the roles later.

- Beware of the title clarity: it happens more often than you would expect: is the meaning of the title clear? Does everyone understand it the same? You can ensure the clarity by defining the responsibilities that you have assigned to the roles. And it is worth it to double-check if everyone in the team understands it.

Conversations To Have

Now that you have a good idea who will be responsible for what in the team, the next step is to decide how you want to manage the business. The points that you will discuss with your cofounders next will be the next input for your last step: documenting it in the cofounder agreement.

Governance

At this point you have chosen who is the leader/CEO and who in the team is responsible for what. Additionally, you also need to answer a few other governance questions. Do you want to have an advisory board? Who will be on the board of directors? Depending on which type of legal entity you choose it will influence which governance bodies you need to have and which are optional. Get the information on what you need and discuss with your team the implications and the initial members of the governance bodies. Depending on the ambition and size of your business, you might consider having an advisory board even when it is optional only to get the additional expertise or industry connections on board. One size does not fit all and no one knows better than you – it is the awareness of the option that gives you the tools to decide well.

Decision making

You also want to define how you will make decisions as a team. Some of the decision making could be defined by law, for the special company type that you choose. Some might not. It is best to know and discuss which type of decisions you want the cofounders to be able to do independently and for which decisions you want to utilise the collective wisdom – and how. Many prescribed templates for shareholder agreements will have a set framework to fill:

- Voting allocation: (default) vote allocation is proportionate to the shareholders' equity share; if nothing else is specified, this voting allocation will apply.

- Which decisions you want to make unanimously or by qualified majority: typically this could be adding a new cofounder, getting an external investor, selling or dissolving the company.

- Which decisions you want to make by simple majority.

- Which decisions you want each cofounder to be able to make independently.

- You might need to define or confirm what is a qualified majority if you use it: typically two-thirds of shareholders.

It is also recommended to define:

- What is the process for decision making: remote, by phone sufficient? Or required in writing? Do you need a formal shareholder meeting and notes?

- Present versus absent voters and how to deal with that.

External liabilities

In the role of a cofounder your business partners could incur liabilities on behalf of the business. What does it mean? They purchase services or products from third parties. What is the threshold where you feel comfortable each cofounder can decide independently? And what happens if they exceed that authorisation? In legal terms, it depends on what is the form of your business – from simple partnership to public liability company – the authority of the partners to the outside world can be by law set differently. Depending on your choice, you will have different options to set the authority. Important is to have the discussion in your team and capture it in your cofounder agreement for the potential damage claim towards your cofounders if they exceed their authorisation.

 Leon and Florian opened a flower shop. They agreed that each partner can independently decide on orders up to 10.000. For the first month, Leon ordered flowers for 25.000 by himself. Unfortunately, the internal liability limitation is not enforceable to third parties. That means that Florian, after he learned about the order, cannot cancel it with the supplier because Leon was not authorised to make the order. He can potentially have a claim against Leon personally for exceeding his authorisation and for the damage to the business. As you can imagine, this is probably not a way to run your business partnership and Florian should probably at this point consider whether he wants to continue the business partnership. If Leon does not have the cash to compensate for the potential damage it might still not help Florian a lot. But it is a whole lot better to have that option and clarity than not.

Milestones and commitment

By now you have defined what each cofounder is committing to the business and what their roles are. The next step is to link the commitment and roles with the milestones for your business. Later (in the chapter on equity allocation) this can be an important element if you either decide for the dynamic equity split or vesting model. In both, the cofounder will get the right to the equity in the business – either directly related to her contribution or based on achieving the set milestones.

The milestones can be defined either as time-based (working x period of time with the business) or task-based (for example acquiring 1,000 users). Use your common sense here; the milestones need to be concrete enough to be able to evaluate whether they are achieved and flexible enough to be adapted if an important part of your business strategy changes as you pivot. Pragmatic, simple and clear is the name of the game. And regularly checking if the milestones reflect the current business strategy is a must.

 Michael, Timo and Jan are developing a platform for gift ideas for clueless boyfriends. One of their targets is to acquire 1,000 users of the platform before raising external investment. The business is at this stage business to customer (B2C). Jan is responsible for this task. In the meantime they get an offer from an external party that wants to invest now – if they customise the platform for businesses i.e. B2B instead. As a team they jointly decide that this is a great opportunity and to change the business strategy. Jan's task is no longer relevant and needs to be updated, partly because his equity vesting is tied to this task. This might happen often and it is one of the reasons why task-based vesting in the early stages has its limits.

It is only now that you are ready to speak about equity allocation of the business. You do not want to know how often I was asked to help cofounders to correct a situation where they start the discussion with potential cofounders by speaking about equity split. And just because it is done often, it does not mean it is right. It is like speaking on the first date about having babies together. Before getting to know each other, before carefully deciding whether you are actually a good match and have broadly similar ideas about how to raise your children. If you would like your cofounding team to be in the minority that survive and thrive, do not move to the next chapter on equity split unless you have checked each of the points on the checklist. You do not make babies unless you are reasonably sure that you want to have them with the other person. Take similar precautions for your business. While it is strongly recommended to follow the seven process steps in the order as described and finish every step before moving to the next one, up until now there was some flexibility. This one is a hard one. Do not move without completing it if you do not want to apply directly for the majority failed partnerships category.

 ## Checklist

- We have defined the cofounding team's roles and individual cofounders' responsibilities.

- We agree as a team how we govern, manage, operate and decide in the partnership.

- We have defined main milestones and commitment for each cofounder.

- All arrangements are clear and understood by each cofounder.

THERE IS A RIGHT EQUITY SPLIT FOR EVERY BUSINESS

06

Split the equity

#1 Decide on equity split   **#2** Split the equity
» Dynamic split
» Fixed split ⟨ Equal
              Unequal

In this chapter we will go through a lot!

- What happens and what you should take care of as soon as you start working with someone else on your business idea.

- When is the right time to talk about equity split?

- What options do you have for allocating/splitting equity?

- Fixed equity splits: equal versus unequal, automatic equity splits calculators, vesting.

- Dynamic equity split: introduction on how it works, pros and cons, further reference if you decide to use it.

Voilà! The right time to speak about equity ownership has arrived. Why only now?

- Because without understanding the role of each of your cofounders in the team you might get it wrong.

- Because without testing each of your cofounders to check that they are true cofounders you might not want to give them equity of your business, or a very different amount of it.

- Because without knowing if you are aligned with your selected future cofounders on the purpose and vision for the business you might not have sufficient base to work together.

In the same time, you want to have this discussion early on before everyone invests significant time or resources into an unclear situation. So yes, it is one of the 1,000+ things you need to be able to handle as soon as you have moved through the previous steps.

Many founders are pushing away the talk about equity split. The reasons can be ranging from prioritising the urgent over the important, to wanting to get more clarity on the cofounders' contributions, to being uncomfortable to raise the question. It is not a good idea and there are no good reasons to not do it. Equity split is one of the most important decisions you need to make about your future business and one with a very significant impact. So do make it urgent. Waiting until all assumptions potentially determining equity choice are confirmed is in any case too late; we will discuss how to deal with the uncertainty and accommodate the need for flexibility in your equity split. Lastly, if you do not feel comfortable having these conversations within your cofounding team, you have a bigger issue than the pending equity split discussion and I would strongly advise you to revisit the steps in the previous chapters before moving any further with the business itself.

Just Because You Do Not Speak About It Does Not Mean It Is Not Happening

The typical timeline – assuming you start from having an idea – to execution (and not from first getting the team to find the idea) is: you have an idea – you start talking to others about your idea – you start working with others on the idea – and somewhere in this stage you decide to start a business with your selected cofounders.

Timeline

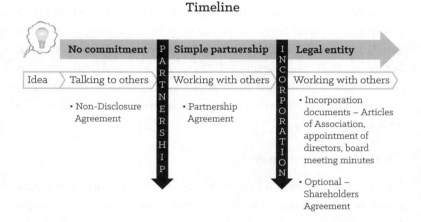

The table summarises the typical legal documents that you should have in place for each stage.

Incorporation means the process of establishing a legal entity which is separate from its owners. The most typical corporations are:

a) Limited liability company

or

b) Public company

Incorporation has many advantages for a business and its owners, including:

1) Protects the owner's assets against the company's liabilities.

    and

2) Allows for easy transfer of ownership to another party.

The time in your startup development matters. Many startup teams get together to work on an idea and develop first a minimum viable product or test feasibility before officially incorporating a company. And it is a good thing! You want to know if your idea has potential before you start cranking up all the administrative and legal costs. But you do want to make sure that the partnership with your partners is clear and fair and that you protect yourself from the existing risks in each stage.

The unaware partnerships

For the stage when you talk to others about your idea, you might consider – depending on the idea – to have a non-disclosure agreement (NDA) with the third parties. However, in practice, especially in the early stages, it is an art to define your idea specifically enough and enforceability of a NDA in reality is a rather tricky topic.

The moment you start working with someone on an idea, in many countries, according to law, you formed a simple partnership. Correct. I know you did not sign anything. I know you maybe did not even yet talk about potentially starting a business together. This can happen by default – automatically – at the moment you start working with someone. And it also does not matter whether you have any customers or whether you have any revenues. My last intention is to scare you *but* my strong objective is to make you an aware founder. It is actually in this time – the time between starting to talk to potential business partners and incorporating the company – that you might be facing the highest personal exposure because in most simple partnerships the partners are fully personally liable for the partnership. What does it mean for you? That you do not want to spend months working with someone else on a potential business idea without addressing your potential partnership and liability.

As I work with startups from Finland to Portugal there are differences between countries on how long this period typically is. Some of the European countries have very minimal capital requirements and costs for starting a company (for example, in both The Netherlands and Portugal it can be done in a very lean way for under 500 euros). Other countries have both higher initial costs and capital requirements (for example, in Switzerland for starting the limited liability company you should reserve between 22,000-25,000 Swiss francs). The lower the threshold, the quicker the teams typically decide to incorporate the company and start the business. The higher, i.e. more expensive, the threshold, the more I see the tendency to work together first, potentially developing the minimum viable product or initial user test, before deciding to incorporate the business.

It is advisable, depending on how long you plan to work together before incorporating a company, to cover the simple partnership period with a solid cofounder agreement.

Unspoken assumptions

Very often people start working together without clarifying what their expectations are from the cooperation. There are a few risks of not speaking about the assumptions including very different expectations of the participants to, later on, one of the participants leaving or being let go without clear agreement on what the compensation is for the work that they did invest in the project.

 Richard has a brilliant idea. And he is a fast mover. He shares the idea with his colleague Rafael and for a few months they are jointly working on it to develop the first prototype of the travel app that Richard had in mind. Then one day Rafael asks him when they will incorporate the company and in that discussion shares with Richard that he expects to be an equal partner in the business. Richard knew that he needed to talk to Rafael about the project but there was always something more urgent that would pop up on the agenda. Now, a few months of joint development work later, he does not share Rafael's opinion about the equal partnership. As I am working with the team through this process, they have a very good chance to find a solution to this dilemma. And even though it might still be salvageable in their case it is rather late to do it. Be aware that in most cases when someone joins you to start work with you on your idea, the chance that they do have an expectation on why they do it is there! And it might be very different from yours. In the case of Richard and Rafael the ideal sequence was to discuss the framework for their cooperation before Rafael joined Richard in the project.

Protecting your idea and intellectual property

Intellectual property is a term being used to refer to 'creations of the mind, such as inventions, literary and artistic works, designs, and symbols, names and images used in commerce'. Intellectual property is protected by law – by patents, design, copyright, trademarks and trade secrets. Some of the available legal protection is applicable automatically (copyright, trade secret), some need to be applied for/ registered (patent, design, trademark).

Typically, the owner of the intellectual property is the creator unless defined otherwise. For example, in an employment relationship it is a frequent clause of the employment contract that any intellectual property developed within the employment relationship is owned by the employer.

IP protection overview

Type	What does it protect	Requirements	How to get it	Duration	Costs
Patent	Technical inventions (NOT software)	New (not publicly available anywhere before) and non-obvious	Filing	20 years	Search 2k Patent application 5-10k US patent 15-28k European patent 20k
Design	Aesthetic appearance of product	New and individual character	Filing 3 years EU protection for unregistered published designs	25 years, renewal fees every 5 years	EU design 2k + 500 renewal fee China 3.5k USA 5k
Trademark	Sign indicating origin for a product / service	Distinctive for registered product / service	Filing	Unlimited	International trademark 5k
Copyright	Text, artistic work, software	Original and results from authors' skill	Automatic (by creation of work)	50/70 years after death of creator	Free
Trade secret	Know how	Information which is more or less secret and gives an advantage over competitors	Protection by secrecy	Unlimited	Free

The purpose of this section is not to make you an expert in intellectual property but to be informed on what it is and what you need to keep in mind when you start to work on your idea with a third party.

There is a very strong sentiment among first-time founders who are afraid to talk to anyone about their idea with a fear that someone might run away with it. There are non-disclosure agreements that you can sign with others with whom you share your idea, to protect it. In practice, they are very difficult to enforce and the risk that someone else will run away with your idea is relatively small. Many seasoned entrepreneurs will share that the world is full of good ideas, it is the execution power that makes the differences, and often the devil is in the detail. There is a difference though between speaking to someone about your idea and getting their feedback and working together with someone on developing the idea. In the second case it might become tricky to distinguish which part of that original idea is yours and which part is the result of the joint efforts. Before you start to work together with someone on your idea you do want to have the framework of your partnership in place. And ideally also a partnership agreement that clearly outlines what will happen with any intellectual property that results from that cooperation. Because not being able to distinguish whether the intellectual property which was originally yours is now shared is a much higher risk than someone running away with your idea.

Fair compensation for contributions from non-cofounders

Another very frequent situation is that people start together to work on an idea without clarifying whether the contribution will be compensated by future equity or cash or not at all.

During the initial cooperation it so happens that one contributor a) is not interested in continuing to build the business to join as a cofounder or b) is not a good fit for the team or business to be invited as a cofounder. So equity compensation is out of the question. Feelings being sometimes hurt – because either the contributor or the company feels rejected – the question of compensation for the work done lands on the table. In the worst case scenario, together with the question about who now owns the intellectual property, I have seen frequently that the rejected cofounder requests compensation for the work she has done based on her regular hourly rates. The company does not agree because it might be at such an early stage that the business has no real value, limited resources and likely the contribution of the rejected cofounder did not bring a whole lot to the development. Finding a fair solution is then very much dependent on the goodwill and the reasonableness of the parties; with hurt feelings in play, this is not the safest bet.

 Sophie invited Laura to join the team developing an integrated fitness platform. Laura's main task was to create a business plan for the company to be used to get the first investors. After three months, when Laura was working on a detailed business plan the team changed its mind and decided to bootstrap the development until the first working prototype and 100+ users. After spending about 150 hours on drafting the business plan, Laura also realised that she did not have the fit with the team and the main cofounder that she expected. She decided to leave and wanted compensation for her 150 hours' work. In that phase, the business was not even incorporated yet and was quite a long way from having the first 100+ users, generating revenue and having a tangible fair market value.

Laura asked for compensation based on the amount of time and her regular consulting hourly rate, amounting to a total claim of €20.000. The team did not agree and was unable to find a mutually acceptable solution with Laura. A few lawyers' consultations later, with each side having incurred costs of about 25% of the total claim, they settled. The total cost of addressing it too late? Cash out for problem solving, a damaged relationship and resources of the fragile early stage project being diverted elsewhere. In their case, the recommended and correct way would have been to agree the framework agreement for the cooperation, also specifying what would happen if Laura did not join the team and if the cooperation gave her right to any compensation in such a case.

When Is The Right Time To Talk About Equity Split

The right time *to talk* about equity split of your future business is right as you start working together with someone. The very practical reasons we outlined above – from having the very real chance that simply by starting to work together you created a simple partnership in terms of law, to avoiding the risk of different expectations having to be resolved later, to protecting any existing intellectual property that you bring into the cooperation. There is a difference between talking and deciding though.

Only after completing steps 3, 4 and 5 – on selecting the best possible cofounder, evaluating if they are true cofounders and knowing and understanding each cofounder's context, working style, alignment of vision and core values – are you ready to make a decision if you want someone to join your cofounding team. And only then it makes sense to talk and *to decide* on the equity split. And yes, that means that you need to move fast if you are eager to start. There is a lot of value in the process itself as equity discussions belong to the more sensitive category. It frequently shows whether you are able to effectively and openly communicate, how aligned your cofounders are on the value of their contribution and how efficient is your team's decision making. And yes, this is also potentially a deal-breaker conversation. If you are not able to agree on an equity split that feels fair and all your cofounders are comfortable with and agree with, it is a very serious reason not to move forward. These discussions typically do not tend to get easier over time. On the contrary.

Important is to avoid the quick handshake solution to get it out of the way, as this usually:

a) Results in a wrong split: too early, without understanding of the cofounders' roles and contribution, typically fixed and with strong bias towards the past and current contributions with less emphasis on the future.

b) Indicates underlying issues in the team to be able to discuss openly sensitive issues: it is not always the case that a longer process leads to better results, but when it comes to equity splits, it is essential to have the open discussion with all cofounders to ensure that they understand the way the equity will be split and agree with it. Any (hidden) doubts will turn very quickly into resentment and potentially serious disruptions of your team as the cofounder who does not feel treated fairly might end up leaving your team.

Risk of doing it too early

Doing it too early here means doing it before you cleared steps 3, 4 and 5 and in such a case there are quite a few items that typically go wrong:

You will have the conversation with candidates that are not true cofounders: they might want to join your business as external contractors or early employees, but they are not prepared to take the risks required to qualify as cofounders.

• You will have the conversation without a clear picture of what is the possible contribution of the person to the business and therefore not having a clear picture of what will be their reward (in the form of equity in the future business).

- You will have the conversation without a clear picture of all the resources you might need to get the business started, therefore allocating too much equity between the current team and not having sufficient reserves for later.

The early business phase is typically very dynamic and uncertain; the risk of fixed equity splits (especially without dynamic components or option to renegotiate) are probably the biggest and most frequent mistake a founding team can make. More on this coming later in the fixed and dynamic equity splits comparison section.

Risks of doing it too late

A few of the risks of doing it too late we talked about earlier – from unspoken assumptions on what the equity split will be, to risking having co-ownership of your intellectual property with someone who might ultimately not be joining your team as a cofounder, to having to find a compensation settlement with a person who contributed some resources in the development stage and will not be joining your team.

Another risk is to lose potentially valuable cofounders who are not willing to accept the uncertainty about the future reward for too long.

The Right Equity Split Depends On Your Situation

There are a few different ways how to split the equity in your future company. Which one is the right one for your business depends on the maturity of your business and your team.

Maturity of your business

Maturity of your business is not necessarily measured in time. It is more a question of how certain you are that you have the *final* (if there is ever something like that in the ever-changing business world anyway) business strategy, *final* pivot round and *final* MVP (minimum viable product, for those who go the lean way). The chance is that at the beginning of your business journey all these three components might have a few rounds of iterations in front of them. Why does it matter? Earlier I mentioned the point that when splitting the equity, founders tend to have the past/current bias (to overestimate the weight of their contribution up until the equity discussion) and underestimate the future ones.

 Remember Michael, Timo and Jan and their gift ideas platform? Initially they thought that their customers would be mainly desperate uninspired boyfriends and husbands, and all of them had a clear role in driving the project from idea to their first goal being 1,000 users, which was Jan's responsibility. As they decided to change the business model from B2C to B2B, not only did Jan's responsibility became obsolete but he was also no longer interested in staying with the team as he did not believe that the new focus would work. Real case, real project, real cofounders.

In the beginning, it is a) very likely that your business strategy/product/service will have a few pivot rounds before you figure it out and b) that the foreseen contribution of your cofounders might change together with those changes! It is no one's fault! And next to knowing that this might happen you need to take it into account when deciding on the equity split between your cofounders.

Maturity of your team

Maturity of your team is not measured by the amount of grey hair in the room or the sum of the days of your team meetings. Or combined years of working experience. Or how many startups you collectively started and successfully exited or failed (and learned from). What I mean by maturity of your team is how well you know each other and if you have worked together before. Watch out for the content and context! The fact that you worked together before as colleagues in your last job, climbed Kilimanjaro, or spent every summer Sunday barbecue together is a very different context from starting a business together. The reason for caution is not only to consider if the skills for which you chose the cofounder are transferable to a different context and environment, but also the uncertainty of how you will work together in the business. I would go as far as to insist that if you have not started a business together before, with similar roles, it is a new situation and therefore has as many uncertainties as if you were creating a team with strangers. This impacts on how early you will be ready to evaluate (ongoing) the contribution of the cofounders to the business and which equity split might be the most suitable for your situation.

 When I started my startup consulting firm with my two ex-colleagues I made a mistake in assuming that we knew how we work together because we had done it before. Before was however in the context of a large international consulting firm, with clear definition of commitment, roles and expertise. We decided to split the equity equally with an idea premium (more on this later). However, the cofounders I selected were not able to make the transition from the corporate way of working to the startup world and despite their unquestionable expertise the team never reached the performing phase and after a few painful months was dissolved. What I failed to see at the time was that despite our previous working experience together and with the different commitment levels, we were an immature team in the new context, and as such a different arrangement – including dynamic component of the equity split and more testing time before – was more suitable.

For my own learning I compared the initial equity split that we had with a recalibrated equity split when the partnership failed. Recalibrated equity split was done using the dynamic equity split based on slicing pie (more on this equity split option coming later) – taking into account contribution of the individual cofounders in the development phase of the project. As you can see, my initial assumption was quite off.

Company equity split

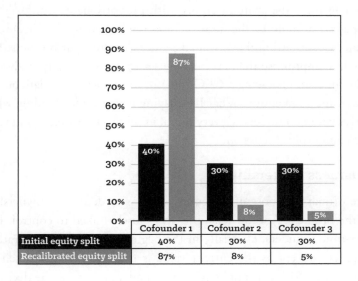

	Cofounder 1	Cofounder 2	Cofounder 3
Initial equity split	40%	30%	30%
Recalibrated equity split	87%	8%	5%

Having had the due diligence discussions of steps 3, 4 and 5 earlier in the process would have made us realise earlier that it would not work, or would have helped us to set up an arrangement that would be fair and sustainable.

The Equity Split Is Not Only About The Business Ownership

Do you remember the oranges story? Where two teams with urgent causes were fighting and overbidding each other to get the only available ton of oranges? And with the help of one smart question they realised that one was after the orange peel while the other was after the orange juice? So they could both have the cake and eat it? There are sometimes similar win-win opportunities in equity discussions. Do you also remember the profit versus control versus impact driver of cofounders?

For some cofounders the main driver is maximising the profit, i.e. the economic aspect of the equity ownership. For some it might be the control – the share of equity with proportionate voting rights. For some it might be the status – for example, getting the CEO role. I am not suggesting that you make a decision for your business that would compromise the best possible set-up for the equity trade-off. Like for example giving a CEO role not to the best candidate but to save some extra equity. What I am saying is that understanding what drives your cofounders is a very useful insight to have before you start the equity split discussion.

Business ownership

The primary purpose of the equity share is to define the ownership of the business. And ownership is very closely linked to control. For first-time founders, especially in the beginning, it could be a rather abstract concept as the current value is uncertain and expected in the future. With this might come the tendency to treat the decision about equity and the resulting ownership rather lightly. This risk is even greater in teams where friends or family are cofounding team members.[18] Next to the profit versus control versus impact drivers there is also theory on different purposes of founding an own business. In cofounding teams with friends and family, the social logic – putting the relationship first – dictates different considerations for the equity split than if business logic is the dominant logic. For business logic, what matters – especially if the equity is being used as reward for the cofounders to invest first – is the contribution of the individual cofounders to the future business.

---

18   Wasserman, N. (2012). The Founder's Dilemmas, p. 194-196. Princeton & Oxford, USA: Princeton University Press

Some famous examples of initial equity splits gone wrong, and substantial amounts of resources – be it time, money and relationship – going to waste include:

Apple: In the initial Apple equity split, both Steve Jobs and Steve Wozniak were having one third of the company. As their different values separated their ways as Apple grew, Wozniak's father indicated that Steve W should have had more equity as it was him who invented the personal computer. Jobs' answer was that without him Wozniak would still be an engineer for Hewlett Packard.

Facebook: Mark Zuckerberg's initial equity split with Eduardo Saverin did not hold the growth and development of the company. The legal battle that followed when Mark Zuckerberg attempted to reclaim Eduardo Saverin's equity, including the negative publicity and damaged relationship, is a standard scenario. What is not standard is that the company survived it.

Zipcar: the cofounder of Zipcar, Robin Chase, wanting to avoid lengthy and sensitive discussions, went 50:50 with her cofounder, Antje Danielson, at their very first meeting. The assumptions that led to this proposal – mainly the skills and commitment of her cofounder – soon proved ill-founded. Her cofounder never even joined the startup full-time. In this case the cofounder eventually left and the main cost for Robin was a year of anxiety and a buy-out offer to her cofounder. At one point the company was valued at US$ 1.2 billion. You do the maths on the price of her mistake had she not been able to resolve it early. To this day however, the two initial cofounders do not speak to each other and the story they communicate about the first development stage of the company and their settlement and parting is very different.

I know, that is their story. Yours is unique. Different. Well – try the next exercise to double-check and dig deeper.

Exercise – The Buyout Offer Is Here

As you are embarking on the relatively risky and for sure demanding path of an entrepreneur, a fair assumption is that at least part of your motivation is to create value with your business and in your business. To understand what your equity split means, hypothetically, test what you have in mind. Imagine tomorrow you get an offer to sell your business for 10 million euros/dollars/pounds/francs – whatever currency you think in. And check what the equity split that you have in mind means in financial terms for you and each of your cofounders. Do it. Write down how much you are getting and how much your cofounders are getting. Does it feel right? If for whatever reason it does not, back to the drawing board.

Decision making

Unless agreed otherwise, in most legal systems and standard legal forms of companies, the ownership directly determines the control over the business – which means that the voting rights are proportionate to each cofounder equity share. This can, depending on the situation, be adjusted by the cofounders opting for equal voting rights or assigning veto rights to certain roles (typically CEO or chairman of the board). Awareness of the different options and also awareness of what your proposed equity split (if you suggest fixed split) means later on – for example by deciding on investors or exit strategy – is another useful exercise. Do keep in mind that if you expect to raise external investment your initial equity share will dilute (become less) in the future, so you might not be able to keep your majority control stake with which you are starting. Before confirming, if you want to deviate from the standard voting rights proportionate to share, check with your local lawyer what is possible.

Motivation

Assigning equity in your company to cofounders also has the motivational element to it: if people have direct benefit from growing the business and creating value they will be more motivated. For making sure that you use the motivational element of equity, you want to include some dynamic elements in your equity split. We will discuss the different options you have later in more detail. It is important to realise that a future slice of the pie (or dangling carrot) is a more powerful motivator then the proverbial bird in the hand.

 One of my clients joined a promising startup team which was developing a travel game: you upload a picture and the users can participate in a competition guessing where it is and what it is. The idea guy identified who he needed on the team to move from idea to prototype and the goal was to move on quickly to raise investment. Business plan and strategy clear. After assembling the team and splitting the equity, with a large premium for the idea guy, he became absent, fully letting the other cofounders 'run with it' and work on it! The project lasted four months and the team has split after winning a prestigious design award and being shortlisted for an accelerator because they were not able to renegotiate the initial equity split and the other cofounders did not feel motivated to continue working on the project.

Selecting The Right Equity Split Is A Life Or Death Question. No Kidding

Equity allocation

The reward – the share of equity your cofounders get – is an essential element to get right. There are a few famous examples where, usually after a lengthy and costly legal battle, the companies survived and thrived despite their initial wrong split. Many more examples, like the promising travel game startup and countless others, are unfortunately skeletons on the majority failed businesses graveyard. The starting point is to know which options you have and can consider, and then choosing the one that best fits your team and context. The main decision is between the fixed versus dynamic equity split and then, of course – the devil being in the detail – how the method is applied in your team. It is said that a team has succeeded at splitting the equity if all of the cofounders are equally unhappy.[19] The equity recovery framework – what happens if a cofounder leaves a team – is an equally important aspect which will be discussed later.

Equal versus unequal equity allocation

Typical examples of equal splits are for two founders 50:50, for three founders 33.3% each, for four founders 25% each and so on. The mathematics of equal splits is the easy part. The difficult one is to make them work. The equal splits are more common in friends/family cofounders' teams where the social logic – putting the relationship first – overrides the business logic. If the main purpose of your business is to do something fun with the people you like and the growth, success or profitability of the business is not that important, carry on. However, if your main objective is to maximise the potential growth and value of your business, it is time to pause and reflect.

The 50:50 split is, in most cases, a very bad idea because of the decision-making deadlock that it causes. But in general even the other equal equity splits which do not cause a similar decision-making deadlock are not a great idea. In reality it is extremely rare to have a situation where all cofounders are contributing equally to the business. The primary problem with equal equity splits is that they are inherently not reflecting the reality and are therefore wrong. Moreover, the equal decision splits could indicate to the outside world either

19 Hellmann, N. W. (2017, April 24). The Very First Mistake Most Start-up Founders Make. Harvard Business Review. Retrieved July 23, 2017, from https://hbr.org/2016/02/the-very-first-mistake-most-startup-founders-make

inexperience of the cofounding team or their inability to address and resolve sensitive issues. That said, there are also cultural conditioning assumptions that might influence the cofounder's preference. Typical for example for the Nordic countries in Europe, where equality is a very strong principle, is the tendency to go for equal splits. Awareness is a key here. The purpose of equity split is not to reflect the value of the cofounders independently but fairly reflect their contribution to the development of the business. We are not all the same and the same applies to individual cofounders' contributions to business.

If you are considering external financing at the later stage of your business, your equal equity split – if you still decide on one – is likely to raise questions. And unless your business is one of the very rare cases where all cofounders do really contribute equally to the business, you might be asked to adjust the equity split later. Statistical research by Professor Noam Wasserman confirmed, controlling for other variables, that 'companies that have equal splits have more difficulties raising outside finance'.[20] And the sensitivity of the equity split topic and later adjustments, when not expected, is more difficult to deal with than right at the start.

Unequal equity allocation

If you decide for an unequal equity split, the next million dollar question is how to split it? If you want your cofounding team to be motivated and sustainable, the equity split needs to fairly reflect the cofounder's contribution to the business. That is easier said than done, but before we panic about all the wires of the parachute, let us start with introducing all the options that you as a cofounder have.

---

20   Hellmann, N. W. (2017, April 24). The Very First Mistake Most Start-up Founders Make. Harvard Business Review. Retrieved July 23, 2017, from https://hbr.org/2016/02/the-very-first-mistake-most-startup-founders-make

The main options you have are:

a) Fixed equity split

b) Dynamic equity split

Fixed Equity Split

Fixed equity split is a split where, at a certain point in time, you cut the pie and distribute the slices and that's it. In a world where you can know upfront that the slices truly and fairly represent the cofounders' past, current and future contribution, it would also be the most logical split. The main weakness of this solution, however, is that the world is constantly changing, therefore the contribution of your cofounders – whether due to their commitment or to the change in the business – will most likely change as the business grows. So the chance – especially if you fix too early (and for good reasons you do not want to fix too late) – is that the slices of the pie will not be fairly representing the cofounders' contribution a few weeks/months/years down the line. We later examine how you can mitigate part of this risk with including vesting schedules, but let us park the time element for now. The best candidates for fixed equity splits are mature teams with mature business plans and ideally in an industry which is not fast-moving (as this can shuffle the cards even for those). There are different methodologies and advices on how to split the equity in this scenario. Most of them will consider one or a combination of the following factors:

• **Commitment and risk contribution**: there is a significant difference in the risk taken between cofounders who work for the startup full-time without salary and cofounders who typically keep their day jobs and agree to only join the startup when the cash flow is secured and sufficient to pay their salary. The part-time cofounder being common if there is *no* risk involved may not be a true cofounder. For the many shades of grey in between, the equity allocation should reflect that the risk is proportionate to the reward. If one or more cofounders take higher risk than the others this should be reflected in the fixed equity split allocation between them.

- **Cash contribution**: cash is king and even more so in the typically cash-starved early stages business phase. Again – risk proportionate to reward – differences between cofounders' cash contribution should be reflected in the equity allocation. However, splitting the equity proportionally *only* to cash contributions is ignoring all the other relevant aspects and likely not reflecting the full big picture. If any of your cofounders is contributing cash only, and no other involvement in the business is foreseen, she is more likely an early stage investor and not a cofounder. You might want to treat her role and contribution as investor only, considering different options to structure her investment (convertible loan for example).

- **Role – CEO premium**: some formulas suggest including in the equity allocation a CEO premium – ranging typically between 5-15% for the CEO. As with other fixed equity attributes, the problem with this one potentially is that at the beginning it might not yet be proven that the CEO is the most suitable person and how much value she will contribute and how long she will be the CEO. Any automatic premium assigned upfront could be off. And often is. Just keep it in mind. Also, once you start allocating premiums for assuming certain roles in your business you are potentially opening very subjective discussions about if the other C-roles qualify for a premium as well and how much the premium should be.

- **Idea premium**: similar to the CEO premium and even more common is to allocate an idea premium. Especially in the case of first-time entrepreneurs, there is a strong bias to overvalue the idea. Many serial entrepreneurs (and investors) share the opinion that whilst ideas are plentiful, it is the skilled execution that is scarce – and value creating. Some type of premium for the idea is, however, widely accepted so you might want to at the minimum consider it. Also, if in the future the idea significantly changes (by a few pivot rounds) the question is whether the idea premium is still justified and feels fair to the whole team. The idea premium also applies if any of your cofounders joins the business with already existing intellectual property; for example, if she has been developing the idea for a few months before forming a team, it might command some type of equity premium. Here it is much more difficult to indicate standard ranges, as it very much depends on how much value is created – i.e. is being contributed to the venture.

There are two main ways to allocate the idea premium. One is by adding (similar to the CEO premium) a fixed percentage to the idea person. The common range is between 5-25%. The second way is to agree on a royalty on the future generated revenues. This is a bit more complex, potentially requiring assistance of a startup lawyer to set it up and might not be suitable for early stage bootstrapping. It is also more suitable for clearly identifiable IP such as patents and more common in the biotech or tech industry with clear future revenue streams already defined.

- **(Startup) experience:** any type of experience and expertise that the cofounders bring to the table is part of their contribution to the business. There seems to be one area that does stand out above the others and that is the very specific experience with starting, growing and selling a business. This experience seems to be valued and frequently results in an equity premium being allocated to the cofounder who brings this experience. The empirical observations in Europe are confirming this trend. The extra equity depends very much though on how the team values this experience and whether it includes the full cycle (from starting the business to exit). For a small business owner starting a local barber shop this might be less relevant than to a high growth fin-tech startup.

- **Industry expertise:** industry expertise is another consideration in equity splits. Having a cofounder with specific industry expertise can often save the business a few pivot iterations. How much it is worth is dependent on the type of business and the business plan. The main questions to consider when deciding on the importance of the industry expertise are: Are you replicating a successful concept or going for industry disruption? How fast and aggressive is your growth strategy? How available is the industry information and know-how to an outsider? Again, it is a part of the cofounder contributions so only the very specific and rare ones should be considered for premium allocations.

- **Network access:** network access can include access to potential investors, distribution channels, high-quality future employees or direct customers. Similarly to the other points, the value will be dependent on the type of business and business strategy that you want to pursue. Questions to consider include: Can you gain access to the network otherwise? How much direct revenue/cash value can access to the network generate for the business? Did you verify the quality of the connections?

Automatic equity calculators

There are quite a few free fixed equity allocation calculators available online. The biggest issue with these is that it is still a snapshot at a particular point in time, fairly superficial and without taking into account the specifics of your business. When you test a few of them, you will reach very different results for the same team depending on which calculator you use, as they give different values to different contributions. Depending on who built the calculator, it may take a quantitative approach with a specific industry focus: if you are a biotech startup your IT contribution is less important than a fin-tech company. Yes, I am a strong believer in standardising and simplifying where possible. However, splitting equity in your business is not a trivial undertaking and one size does not fit all. Importance of the individual elements is very dependent on your industry, geography and business strategy. The advice would be to use it as a starting point and orientation, not as an ultimate decision oracle.

 You can find as your starting point some of the online equity allocation calculators in the resource section on cofounding.info.

Whichever methodology is adopted, a major weakness of the fixed equity split remains that it is extremely difficult to choose the timing which is both not too late and when there is sufficient clarity about the cofounders' contribution assumptions, and the fact that most of them prove to be wrong when later evaluated by looking at the cofounders' actual contributions. And just because it is a majority solution it does not mean it is the best one!

> ## "The most common ways in which founders split equity is also the most hazarduous one."
>
> Dr. Noam Wasserman

Another weakness is that once the equity is allocated, you might end up – worst case but not an uncommon scenario – with cofounders who are owning equity and not contributing (remember the travel app story?). To some extent, vesting – coming next – can help to mitigate part of this risk. If you decide to go for fixed equity split, *always* combine it with vesting schedules!

Vesting

What exactly is vesting? It is nothing else than saying that the right to the equity in the business which was agreed between the cofounders will be acquired either a) over time and/or b) with reaching set milestones.

Time-based vesting

It is this aspect of your fixed equity split that helps to mitigate the risk of cofounders leaving the business after a few months with their full equity share (a more common real life scenario than you would want to know) and also helps to keep the cofounders motivated.

The typical time vesting is structured over a period of between two and four years. It can be divided proportionately (allocated shares divided over the vesting period) and executed in set periods (quarterly, monthly). It is also popular to include a cliff – an initial period before the vesting will become effective and enforceable. If you agreed to include the four years proportionate vesting schedule with one year cliff, you will get the first quarter of your agreed equity share only after the first 12 months. Cliffs are basically equivalent to the probation time in an employment relationship and allow you a time-limited trial period where the cofounders work together and can further test if they are a fit. If any cofounder decides to leave within the cliff period, time-based vesting prevents you having tiny equity pieces allocated between many shareholders which makes the future legal work much more complex and does not give you extra points with future investors.

Acceleration is another feature sometimes used, typically for advisors or board members. It means that if a specific trigger event occurs (the most common being an exit), the vesting is accelerated, meaning the full agreed equity shares become fully vested at the moment the event is happening.

 This is what a practical example looks like: Jana, Maria and Katherina started a fashion company and agreed a four-year vesting period with one year cliff with the following split: Jana 50%, Maria 20%, Katherina 20%, 10% was reserved for the future employees fund. The company was sold in year 3.

This is how their equity ownership looks like over time:

Shares vesting and cliff example

Equity share without company sale						
	Fixed equity split	Y0	Y1	Y2	Y3	Y4
Jana	50%	0.0%	12.5%	25.0%	37.5%	50.0%
Maria	20%	0.0%	5.0%	10.0%	15.0%	20.0%
Katherina	20%	0.0%	5.0%	10.0%	15.0%	20.0%

Equity share with company sale (and acceleration)						
	Fixed equity split	Y0	Y1	Y2	Y3	Y4
Jana	50%	0.0%	12.5%	25.0%	50.0%	
Maria	20%	0.0%	5.0%	10.0%	20.0%	
Katherina	20%	0.0%	5.0%	10.0%	20.0%	

The main limitation of time-based vesting is potential underperformance of cofounders. I know that no one wants to think in the beginning that after all the due diligence and research you did (back to steps 3, 4 and 5) to select the best possible cofounders team that it could happen that any of your cofounders will not deliver and will underperform. But famously and succinctly put by Maya Angelou: 'Hope for the best, prepare for the worst and know that anything in between can happen.'

Being prepared for the possibility that any of your cofounders will not deliver what the team agreed and believed when you were splitting your equity is not a sign of distrust in the team. It is a sign of sensible and responsible team leadership. I do agree that it is frequently loaded with negative taste – similar to prenuptial agreements of couples getting married. Sometimes I wonder who is doing all the negative lobbying behind the scenes. Because the one and only intention for being prepared for break-ups is that should that unfortunate event happen, you will not spend years in court rooms and a fortune on lawyers to deal with it. And if the marriage success rate is around 50% and business partnerships around 30%, it is insanity not to prepare for the fact that there is a real chance that this might happen in real life. And of course, do your very best to ensure that it does not happen.

Unfortunately, pure time-based vesting – without combination with milestones or specific agreements on performance – is not protecting you for the case that the cofounder is staying with the business but not delivering, with her contribution not as valuable as your initial equity split assumed.

Milestones-based vesting

Milestones-based vesting is far less common then time-based vesting and is often used in combination with time-based vesting. In the US, about 10% of startup ventures that use vesting use a milestones-based one. The milestones-based vesting could in theory be very powerful to address the performance/motivation. In the dynamic changing world, which is even more pronounced in early stage business ventures, the challenge is how to define the milestones concretely but flexibly enough and what to do if they are no longer relevant.

 Do you remember Michael, Timo and Jan developing a platform for gift ideas for clueless boyfriends? They defined as one of their next targets to acquire the first 1,000 users of the platform in the next six months, with Jan being responsible for this task and 25% of his equity share vesting being tied to this task. As they decided to change their model to B2B (business to business) and offer the app to financial institutions as an interesting feature for their clients, the milestone of the first 1,000 customers in the next six months became completely irrelevant. As they were a lean team with good communication and no external shareholders and investors, they could set a new milestone and continue. Their experience just illustrates the limitation of milestone-based vesting in early stage ventures.

Similar situations can lead to lengthy discussions and in one case I even witnessed the break-up of the cofounding team. The point is, your business strategy might change. You do not want to have milestones defined in a way that you need to renegotiate and change them frequently. If your business strategy is final, stable and you are able to define the milestones flexibly enough, by all means combine it with your time vesting. Just be aware of the pitfalls.

Reversed vesting or re-vesting

Reversed vesting is not something that is necessarily relevant for you when you do the initial equity split with your cofounders but could become relevant later. It is sometimes required by investors to secure their investment against key team members leaving. It means that even after your cofounding team is fully vested – i.e. have all acquired their full share of the business's equity – it can be reversed. Sometimes it is a condition of the investor to request reversed vesting, meaning that the cofounders' team will have to 'regain' the shares over a new set vesting period. It is an investor's insurance against key cofounders leaving after their investment and by that increasing the startup's risk.

Final thoughts on fixed equity splits

The fixed equity split is widely accepted and almost universally practised. And it is surely to a big extent responsible for the high failure rate of business partnerships, especially where the maturity of the team and the business is not quite there yet. And no, it is not because in the beginning someone wants to take advantage of the others (most often). It is mainly due to the fact that it is close to impossible to predict how the future will be and many assumptions for the equity splits are based on future expectations. Vesting is partially mitigating some of the main weaknesses of the fixed equity split, but only partially. Time-based vesting helps to motivate the cofounders to stick around but time alone is a weak proxy for value creation and performance. Milestones-based vesting requires highly structured project plan estimation in a very dynamic business stage and risks not getting the milestones definition right beyond the short term.

Dynamic Equity Split (DES)

Is there not a better way? Given all the challenges of fixed vesting, one of the increasingly popular alternatives is the dynamic equity split. It can either be dynamic by cofounders agreeing to renegotiate and verify their initial split later or, for a certain period, it can be dynamic by construction. By far the most comprehensive dynamic equity split method is the Slicing Pie method developed by Mike Moyer. For early stage bootstrapped startups (for whom it is developed), it is considered the fairest equity split.[21]

---

21 Moyer, M. (n.d.). Perfect Equity Splits for Bootstrapped Start-ups. Retrieved July 30, 2017, from http://slicingpie.com/

How does it work? Using the metaphor of baking a pie, you get a team together to make a pie and everyone on the team is promised a piece of the pie once the pie is baked. In the beginning, you did not even decide yet which pie you are going to bake. Is it going to be an apple pie? Chocolate brownie? Carrot cake? And who has the best recipe? And the main ingredients? Who can spend most time preparing the dough? The advantage of dynamic equity split is that it is OK not to have all the answers. You start baking the pie and just record the contribution of each baker. Before the pie goes into the oven, you calculate how large a piece of the pie goes to which baker based on how much she *actually* – not *expectedly* – contributed to the baking.

- For who: for startups that are using sweat equity to reward their cofounders for investing their resources.

- For when: it is from as early as the team starts to work together until there is either sufficient cash flow to pay the cofounders for their work (by external investment or the business achieving sufficient profitability) or by agreement of the cofounding team to fix (because there is sufficient clarity and stability to do it).

The basic philosophy behind Slicing Pie is that when someone contributes to a startup company and is not paid in full for her contribution, she is at risk of never being paid. She is, in effect, 'betting' on the future value created by the company. The amount she bets is equal to the unpaid portion of the fair market value of her contribution. Her share of equity, therefore, should logically be based on her share of the bets.

Every person who contributes and is not getting paid is betting. Every day people place more bets in terms of money, time, relationships, facilities, supplies etc. Betting continues until the company breaks even or raises financing. At those points the betting typically stops because everyone can be paid for their contribution from then on.

It is impossible to know in advance how much betting will be required before (sufficient) value is created, but by keeping track of the bets you will always know the fair split for when it happens. In the Slicing Pie model, the contributions are tracked using a fictional unit of at-risk contribution called a 'slice'. There is no end to how many slices a pie can have. At any given time the formula below will calculate a cofounder's fair share:

Cofounder's equity = Cofounder's slices/all slices

The Slicing Pie formula is straightforward, simple and comprehensive. It includes all potential contributions that cofounders can bring to the table, dividing it into cash and non-cash categories. It measures the cofounders' contributions over time and dynamically adjusts the equity ownership according to the accumulated contributions.

Below is a basic explanation of the dynamic equity split based on the Slicing Pie method by Mike Moyer. The purpose of the section is informative – for you to learn about the option. In case you decide that it is suitable for your business, Mike Moyer developed many useful materials around his method that you can use. As the devil is again in the detail, read the implementation.

Equity allocation framework

The main underlying principle is: everyone gets what they deserve, no more and no less, and the share of the reward is directly proportionate to the share of the risk. What is at risk is being measured by quantifying the fair market value of all the contributions that the individual cofounders bring to the table.

It measures the cofounders' contributions over the set period of time. When the 'pie goes in the oven', the business is ready to fix the equity and the equity will be allocated to each of the cofounders fairly, based on their actual contributions. The framework allows for the addition of new cofounders later on fairly easily too. I would remind you on making sure that they are true cofounders and that you really need them; remember every additional cofounder does exponentially increase the complexity. At one point I was contacted by a startup who at that time had over 40 cofounders in the pie. That is clearly not a way to go. But if you do need to add, the DES enables you to plug the new cofounder in – either starting from zero or accounting for any initial contribution he brings – and start working.

The formula distinguishes two main contribution categories:

- Cash: cash and unreimbursed expenses.

- No-cash: time, ideas, relationships, customers, investors, partners, employees, facilities.

To be able to equally measure them – and based on that measurement, to compare the individual cofounders' contributions – the resource invested is a function of the fair market value of the contribution and a risk multiplier. The cash multiplier is higher than no cash contributions and any cash invested is counted as a contribution only once the money is actually spent. The risk multipliers are in principle variable, but I would strongly recommend sticking with the method as it was developed – and tested. The Slicing Pie method recommends a cash multiplier of four and non-cash multiplier of two.

The cofounder contribution is calculated as the fair market value of her contribution x multiplier (cash or non-cash).

The most frequent cofounder contribution is time. One of the inputs is to agree on the fair market value of the cofounders' time. This discussion alone is a very good check if the cofounding team has similar opinions about the approximate value of each other's contributions.

The fair market value of cofounders' time contribution = hours spent x hourly rate x non-cash multiplier

The formula is very simple, comprehensive and clear. The *Slicing Pie Handbook* provides details and information on how to implement it – from valuation of the individual contribution categories, to setting the input parameters, to what happens if a cofounder leaves (the equity recovery framework), to changing to fixed equity split, typical legal issues, how to retrofit (in case you would like to switch to dynamic equity split) and forecast.

 If the fashion company example with Jana, Maria and Katherina had used the dynamic equity split, they would have found this out. The initial assumption on the equity stake of the first three cofounders was: Jana 50%, Maria 20%, Katherina 20%, with 10% reserved for the future employees' fund. As the products of the company got very popular in China, which was not the initial expectation or business plan, it so happened that the contribution of Katherina, who had a distribution network in China that helped to grow the sales beyond their expectations, was much more valuable than her initially foreseen role.

The summarised contributions of the cofounders based on the Slicing Pie method look like the following:

Fashion co DES

Slicing Pie   **FASHION COMPANY**

Theoretical Vaule of Fund	$	725'000

	Jana	Maria	Katharina
Time	$ 250'000 $	95'000 $	200'000 $
Cash	$ 35'000 $	25'000 $	- $
Equipment and Supplies	$ - $	- $	- $
Facilities	$ - $	- $	- $
Intellectual Property	$ - $	- $	- $
Commissions	$ - $	- $	120'000 $
Total	**$ 285'000$**	**120'000$**	**320'000$**

	Jana	Maria	Katharina
Slice of the Pie	39%	17%	44%
Equity share (recalculated from the slice)*	**35%**	**15%**	**40%**

*only 90% equity split between cofounders

The value of the cofounders' contribution, which was in the early development stage mainly their time and cash, gets recalculated to its theoretical value (based on the fair market salary and hours worked multiplied by two for the time and multiplied by four for the cash) to allocate the pie slices. The pie slices are then recalculated (keeping the same proportion) to the 90% equity that the cofounders are splitting between themselves. The 10% is reserved for the early employees. If the cofounders have 100% equity allocated for themselves the pie slices will be equal to their individual equity share.

Check the equity split difference:

Equity split comparison

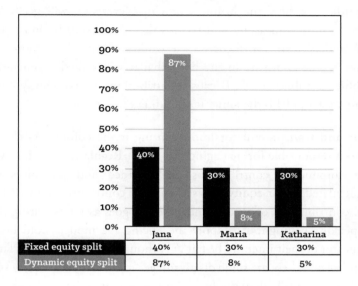

	Jana	Maria	Katharina
Fixed equity split	40%	30%	30%
Dynamic equity split	87%	8%	5%

As you can see, the differences in the individual cofounder shareholdings at the time the company was sold are very significant. It was mainly due to the rather unexpected expansion in China that the company was successfully sold. Katherina played a significant role in the Chinese expansion. In the initial fixed equity split her contribution was estimated without the Chinese expansion, and based on that she was allocated 20% equity. If her equity share had been based on the actual contribution by the time the company was sold, it would have been double – 40%.

Why I believe dynamic equity split is the best thing since sliced bread

The dynamic equity split addresses many of the problems in the minefield of fixed equity splits. As Mike Moyer puts it, it is a new way to think about a very old problem.

No need for future telling: it is not asking the cofounders the impossible – to have a crystal ball and look into the future on what their contributions will be. It is simply saying start working and, regardless of how the business develops, everyone will get a fair slice because it measures and records the actual contributions. Your cofounders' team can focus on the work and contribute more and more to the company in the hope that it will someday generate a profit, go public or sell. Because contributions are constantly being made, the model is dynamic. It self-adjusts to stay fair.

Fair and transparent: for implementing it the cofounders choose who is responsible for managing the 'fund'. Regularly at set intervals the cofounders' contributions are recorded and pie slices are recalculated. Their equity is based on their contributions divided by the contributions of all cofounders. Mike goes as far as stating that 'a person's willingness to apply the Slicing Pie model could be an indicator of their intent to be fair'.[22] Although I would not go as far as that because there are some disadvantages to the dynamic equity split and one size really does not fit all, I do agree that at the minimum the unwillingness of any cofounders to use the method should alert you to explore further the reasons why.

Forces value talks: one of the things the cofounders need to agree when they want to implement the dynamic equity split is the relative value of their time contributions – that is to say, their fair market salary. This is *not* the cofounder's last corporate job salary. This is a salary that you would get in a comparable context and environment for your work. The conversation that the team needs to have to set the fair market salary of each cofounder is a very good check on the alignment of the team's expectations. In some (rare) cases, the discussion would make the cofounders realise that they have very different opinions on each other's value that they bring to the table. And that the difference is so significant that they decide not to continue with the business

---

22   Moyer, M. (2016). *Slicing Pie Handbook*: Perfectly Fair Equity Splits for Bootstrapped Start-ups, p. 11. USA: Lake Shark Ventures LLC

project. Painful, yes, and great news at the same time. Because if the cofounders realise it now, it will slow the business or in a worst case scenario mean that the business will not continue – but before there are months or years of invested effort and resources and potentially conflicting opinions on business liquidation.

Introduces structure and discipline: if the time that the cofounders spend on the business is directly influencing their equity share (by the nature of the method) then there is more discipline on measuring the time in relationship to the output and link to the overall business goals. And that does not hurt! – especially in the sometimes rather chaotic way early stage businesses operate.

Simple and comprehensive: the hardest thing in any field is to do complex things in a simple way. And that is what dynamic equity split does: by covering all the possible cofounder contributions – assigning them hypothetical value – and then recalculating the split relative to total contributions, it simplifies the often black box of the fixed equity split calculators. You get x% of the pie because you contributed x% of the value.

Too good to be true?

The method is simple, fair and there are many businesses that used it successfully in the early bootstrapped stages. It is addressing many of the fixed equity issues. And it is either loved or hated.

New means suspicious (to many)

Because it is a new way to address a very old problem, many people view it with suspicion and distrust, with most of them turning into passionate advocates once understanding it. Unlike the old solution though, it is in relatively early stages. There are many future parties that might need to interact with your business who will not be familiar with the method – from investors, to employees, to new cofounders, to tax authorities or even to judges in courtrooms.

Unknown reactions (the authorities)

When talking to Mike Moyer and the team of US lawyers who have been implementing the DES method since 2012 (and before my deciding to invest a lot of time, effort, blood, sweat and tears into developing the templates for continental Europe), I was curious about their experiences in the US, the location where early stage businesses used it the most (until now) and for longest. And I was dumbfounded to hear that we actually do not know because, to our common knowledge, none of the slicing pie/DES businesses ended up in court since 2010, the year when it was born. The bad news is that there is no jurisprudence or case law (knowing how the courts will react if having slicing pie case questions). The good news is that most likely the combination of the simplicity and fairness of the method, together with the complete recovery framework, enables the founders to resolve any upcoming issues using the DES framework itself, without the need to spend their valuable resources in lengthy disputes. The point which remains is that it is a method that not everyone is familiar with and there are many question marks on how the traditional authorities will react when needing to decide on it.

I love it! What do I do next?

The outline of the method is to raise awareness that you – yes, you the founder – have more options to split your equity. And if you happen to be a bootstrapped startup in the early stages the dynamic equity split is likely the best possible option for you. It is not a complete guide on how to apply it.

Moyer has developed great materials about the dynamic equity split, from how to implement it for your business from the start – the *Slicing Pie Handbook* – to how to change your existing equity allocation to dynamic – the Recalibration Guide – and other materials. If you decide that the dynamic equity split is the right solution for you, start with you and your team reading the *Slicing Pie Handbook* to make sure that everyone understands the method fully. Yes, there are shortcuts in life but this is not the occasion when you want to take them.

The DES journey

Thanks to Mike Moyer's effort, openness and absolute dedication to the cause, there are standardised solutions available to implement the dynamic equity split in the US, Canada, Australia, the UK, Switzerland, the Netherlands, Argentina, Mexico, Chile, Uruguay and South Africa. We are now working on having the solution available for France, Germany, Spain, Portugal, Italy, Denmark, Estonia, Czech Republic, Slovakia and Bulgaria.

With the mission of promoting fairness for entrepreneurs, Mike and the team are working hard on developing affordable solutions to implement the dynamic equity split for businesses all over the world.

DES PROJECT UPDATE DECEMBER 2017

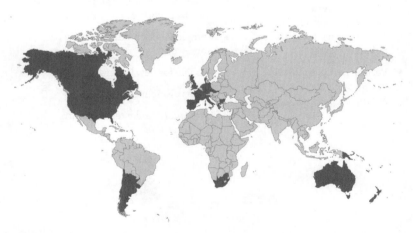

*Highlighted are countries where Slicing Pie is being implemented

Fixed versus dynamic splits

In summary: there is no one size fits all. Both methods have their strengths, time and purpose. What is important for all though is not only to 'get the initial equity split right – by matching it as closely as possible to the founders' past contributions, opportunity costs, future contributions and motivations – it is equally important to keep it right, that is, to be able to adjust the split as circumstances change'.[23]

What I wish for you is to be aware of all the options you have when it comes to making such an essential decision as splitting your equity and making an informed decision what fits the best:

Fixed vs dynamic equity comparison

FIXED EQUITY SPLIT	DYNAMIC EQUITY SPLIT
• Certainty of the cofounders	• Fair - reward (equity share) based on real contributions
• Well known and accepted	• Self-adjusts with the business development
• Stable and predictable	• Well suited for initial stage bootstrap startups
• Almost always not fairly reflecting actual contributions if without dynamic element	• Complete – including recovery framework
• Vesting partial solution for the dynamic element, but has own issues	• Flexible for new joiners
	• Forces discipline
	• New and not fully tested (courts, tax authorities)

---

23 Wasserman, N. (2012). The Founder's Dilemmas: anticipating and avoiding the pitfalls that can sink a start-up, p. 168. Princeton: & Oxford USA: Princeton University Press

Checklist

- I have spent time and attention on the choice of equity split with the cofounding team.

- I have considered the specific nature of the business (industry, geography and business strategy).

- I am aware of the past versus future contributions bias.

- If choosing a fixed equity split, I included a dynamic element (vesting).

- If choosing a dynamic equity split, every cofounder understands and agrees with the method and input parameters.

CHAPTER 7:

IMPLEMENT YOUR COFOUNDER AGREEMENT

07

Cofounders agreement

» Document it
» **LIVE IT**

After this chapter you will understand:

- The different types of legal documents needed.

- Main building blocks for your cofounder agreement.

- Legal contractual essentials (for any type of contract).

- What you need to do beyond signing the agreement.

The Surprising Fact That Standard Legal Templates Do Not Cover All Necessary Cofounder Agreements

Now that you have agreed with your cofounders how to split the equity of your future business, it is time to implement it. There is a widely spread assumption amongst many cofounders that by incorporating the company, the typical required obligatory official documents are somehow taking care of all that is needed. I am with you – it would be very logical to expect it to be as such. Unfortunately, it is not so.

Firstly, the typical incorporation legal documents do not address many of the cofounder relationship aspects automatically. Illogical as it may be, they are only focusing on recording the important agreements (relevant to others) such as equity split and decision making – so if third parties deal with your company they can be informed about your company components that are most relevant for them. Most of them are not automatically dealing with other crucial aspects such as equity recovery framework, good/bad leaver clauses, vesting, agreements on commitment and how you work together, dispute resolution etc.

As you are an informed founder, and went with your team through the steps to define these crucial aspects, you can ask your lawyer to implement it in a cofounder agreement, or do it yourself. I strongly recommend this sequence of steps. If you ask your lawyer to begin with, she will focus on the typical components which are most of the time not covering all the important elements. You are also starting then from the end, instead of going with your cofounders through the very important alignment process which culminates with the cofounder agreement. The cofounder agreement should follow as a result of the discussion, not lead it! You can find these agreements also being called shareholder or partnership agreements. The shareholder agreement is typically used for incorporated companies. Please be aware that in most legal systems it is not obligatory to have one! The partnership agreement will be typically covering the period of developing the idea with the team prior to incorporation of the company.

As the cofounder agreement (in a written form) is not required, the majority of first-time founders do not have one. If they incorporated the company then they will have the equity split and default decision-making rules covered by the incorporation documents, which are not always the best fit for their particular situation. This is not enough!

Documenting Your Agreement is Key

Avoiding the memories battles

Many of the unfortunate, lengthy and expensive legal battles between cofounders are the battles of memories and different understanding. What do I mean? In some cases, at the beginning of their cooperation, cofounders might have talked about some of the aspects of how they work together or what their vision for the company is. When the time comes that this becomes important (and it always comes), they try to recall what was agreed and the only fallback they have is to dig in their memories.

Do we mean the same?

Another typical source of conflict is different understanding. How often does it happen to you in life that you communicate with someone only to find out later that they understood something different? This does not have to have an underlying bad intention. We are all operating with different maps of the world. The information we receive goes through many filters of our minds, which are created by our cultural background, previous experience and opinions. The same information can be – and often is – understood by two individuals very differently.

Leaving such an important part of your business – your relationship with your cofounders – to be reliant on the memory or an unconfirmed understanding is a very risky and expensive option.

Documenting your cofounder agreement in writing is key and gives you quite a few points on the mitigation of the risks associated with a business partnership that fails. Sometimes – especially in teams where some of the cofounders are family or friends – it is avoided for the risk to create an impression that there is lack of trust. As a responsible founder, you do not need to make the same mistakes as others when you can learn from theirs. Not having clarity which is documented is the risky and untrustworthy option.

Clarifies and confirms common understanding

The benefit of putting things in writing is that you need to be able to formulate them very clearly. And when other people read them and are asked to sign them, they either ask some additional questions to verify their understanding, ask you to change it if they understand it differently or confirm that you both understand it in the same way. This is priceless. Many times cofounders think they are perfectly aligned until they have to express their agreement in writing. It does flag the gaps in understanding immediately and allows the team to close the gaps without stakes or emotions being high.

 In my project for a startup consultancy, we decided at the beginning of the idea to get coaching and online courses developing business knowledge. The costs of the coaching and course were about 50% of the total investment that I put into the project and to me it was very clear that it was a joint decision and an investment for the project, where both I and one of the other cofounders participated. When terminating the project a few months later, I was (unpleasantly) surprised when my cofounder was arguing that this cost was a private investment that I should be carrying. Not having any proof of our agreement and understanding, the easiest was to swallow the bitter pill and remember the lesson.

When in doubt – look it up

Yes, it does happen very often that agreements are forgotten in the heat of building a business. And it does save hours of lengthy discussions if you have the map drawn and you only need to align the compass, as opposed to redrawing the map every time you hit a fork in the road. Once you have agreed and documented the essentials, anytime when such a discussion comes up, for the benefit of all you look up what you agreed and continue. I did meet some founders who believed that this was a waste of their valuable time and they needed to be carrying on to build or grow the business instead. The time saved ahead by having it in place is exponential. It is smooth sailing as opposed to the bumpy road of every time going through the alignment again. It is not a question of nice to have; it is a question of when you decide to invest the time at the right moment, as it will save you much more time – and potentially your business – in the future.

Legal benefits of having a proof

I know you do not want to think that it can ever be you. That stuff happens to other people, teams, businesses. Not you. I wholeheartedly wish for you that you are right, and at the same time urge you not to be foolish. Similar to insurance, you hope all that bad stuff never happens, but in case it does, oh how good it is to be covered. Think about it in a similar way: if sailing goes smoothly, you might never need to refer back to your cofounder agreement as proof in a legal battle when you and your cofounders stand on the opposite side. If such an unfortunate event happens though, you all want to have the best and most fair way possible to resolve it by having as proof what you all agreed in a written and signed cofounder agreement. In situations without such an agreement it is very difficult (if not impossible) to decide between two parties telling opposite stories. Important is also to not only write and sign but also archive it so you can find it if you need to refer back to it! [24] Why play Russian roulette? You have more important things to do.

Here Is How You Do It

Talking with many cofounders, I understood that outside of the legal world there is a little bit of confusion on what is where and what covers what. Understandably – because in my humble opinion it is neither very standardised nor practical.

The outline below is a generic one because these things do differ depending on the country in which you are incorporating your company and what type of company it is. The main takeaways from the overview below for you are:

- In most European jurisdictions – even after incorporation – the shareholder (cofounding) agreement is not obligatory. You do not have to have one. But you definitely do want to have one.

- Depending on what is already (typically standard templates) included in your Articles of Association (the incorporation documents), make sure that all the items are covered in your shareholder (cofounding) agreement and partnership charter.

- A cofounding agreement is a binding legal document. A partnership charter outlines how the cofounders wish to work together and the recommendation is to make it a non-binding (because of the soft rules included, it would be hard to enforce it legally) attachment of the cofounding agreement. The advantage of attachment is that if you need to change it, you can do it by amending the attachment only without touching the cofounding agreement.

---

24 Cofounder agreement: the typical terminology is partnership agreement prior to incorporation and shareholder agreement after incorporation

Timeline infographics with documents

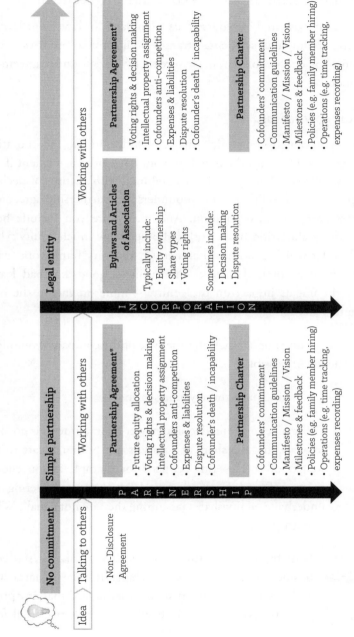

| Idea | No commitment | Talking to others | Simple partnership | Working with others | Legal entity | Working with others |

No commitment

Talking to others

- Non-Disclosure Agreement

Simple partnership

Working with others

PARTNERSHIP

Partnership Agreement*
- Future equity allocation
- Voting rights & decision making
- Intellectual property assignment
- Cofounders anti-competition
- Expenses & liabilities
- Dispute resolution
- Cofounder's death / incapability

Partnership Charter
- Cofounders' commitment
- Communication guidelines
- Manifesto / Mission / Vision
- Milestones & feedback
- Policies (e.g. family member hiring)
- Operations (e.g. time tracking, expenses recording)

Legal entity

INCORPORATION

Bylaws and Articles of Association

Typically include:
- Equity ownership
- Share types
- Voting rights

Sometimes include:
- Decision making
- Dispute resolution

Working with others

Partnership Agreement*
- Voting rights & decision making
- Intellectual property assignment
- Cofounders anti-competition
- Expenses & liabilities
- Dispute resolution
- Cofounder's death / incapability

Partnership Charter
- Cofounders' commitment
- Communication guidelines
- Manifesto / Mission / Vision
- Milestones & feedback
- Policies (e.g. family member hiring)
- Operations (e.g. time tracking, expenses recording)

Essential elements of the cofounder agreement

You can choose to do it yourself, use templates, or have your lawyer, spouse, friend or an accidental stranger do it for you. But irrespective of how you choose to do it, make sure that your cofounder agreement includes:

Equity ownership

For incorporated companies this is included in the incorporation documents. Flesh out the details in your cofounder agreement if the equity split is either dynamic or combined with vesting. Especially important is to codify this for cofounders in a partnership agreement before company incorporation. And make sure you include both the equity allocation framework (who gets how much equity when and under which conditions) and equity recovery framework (what happens if a cofounder leaves the business, good and bad leaver scenario and its impact on the equity) – more on this in the next chapter.

Depending on your country and the type of the company, you might also include if possible:

- Different equity and revenue sharing

- Different equity and decision power – sometimes it is possible to agree that the share of equity is not proportionate to the weight of votes – this happens for example if you choose a one cofounder one vote model without considering the underlying equity shares (assuming they are not equal). What does that mean?

 Four founders – Jasmin, Eva, Marta and Lea – started a business. Jasmin has 40% ownership, Eva 25%, Marta 20% and Lea 15%. For the first year they agreed that any profit the business makes will be split equally between all four founders – each gets 25% of the profit for the year even though their equity share is not equal. On top of that, they also decided that each founder has one vote, with Jasmin having a veto if they are deadlocked (for example, if Jasmin and Lea are for a decision and Marta and Eva against it, Jasmin's vote decides).

Equity - profit - voting split*

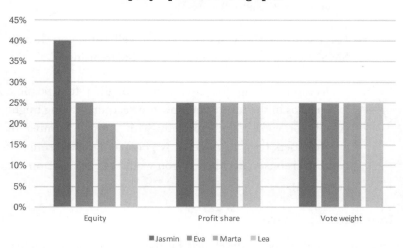

* the possibility to have different voting rights to shares depends on the company legal form and jurisdiction

Decision making

Most commercial laws provide default rules for decision making. You want though to think proactively about this and choose the best fitting for your team and business.

A few decisions that you will be making in the future include:

- Is the voting power proportionate to equity share?

- For which decisions do you want the cofounders to agree unanimously (all of you)? – it could be for example dissolution of the business, accepting a buy-out offer, or adding of a new cofounder.

- For which decision do you want the cofounders to agree by majority? And is it qualified majority (typically two-thirds) or simple majority (more than half)?

- For voting do you request all cofounders to be present? How do you treat the absent votes?

- For recording the votes is a phone call sufficient? Email? SMS? Record in any team tools that you are using?

 Decision-Making Exercise: run through a few possible scenarios in the future and how the decision making might look for your team; especially with a small number of cofounders (two to three) it is good to simulate some of the decisions to decide how you would like to agree on the majority.

Intellectual property

Any intellectual property developed by the team or any individual cofounder during her participation in the business shall be the ownership of the business (whether a partnership before incorporation or the company after incorporation). Unless you explicitly agreed, you have a risk of a cofounder leaving with a critical part of the future business growth and replicating it elsewhere, or at the minimum an unclear intellectual property ownership situation ahead.

Competition agreement

Similarly, when a cofounder leaves you might want to agree certain limitations on how and when the leaving cofounder can potentially start doing the same business – elsewhere or with/without someone else. This could include not only protection of the intellectual property but also that the leaving cofounder will not take the existing employees or customers. Reasonableness of this clause very much depends on the context; if you are starting a consulting firm it is not realistic to ban your cofounders from continuing in what is their main specialisation if they decide to leave your business. However, if you are developing an innovative and new concept, the ban to reproduce it somewhere else is not unreasonable.

Expenses and liabilities limitation

Depending on what you agreed, you might need to define how the team is recording expenses and how and whether they are reimbursed. If they need to be agreed before and jointly, how will that work? Email enough? SMS enough? Phone call? And what is the response time that you need from the team for realistically using this option?

 One of my clients agreed with her cofounder that for any expense above 100 euros they both needed to decide jointly. As the initial phase required quite a few business trips by the cofounder, this proved to be a very impractical requirement that they had to change very early on.

Think ahead and think in a way that will not paralyse your business operations but still give you sufficient control and checks for what you agreed.

Dispute resolution

There are shades of grey and there are scales of disagreement and it is good to agree with your team how you want to handle conflict when it occurs. Do you set a time limit for resolving the issue internally first? Do you, as a next step, agree to choose a third party neutral mediator to help you? Do you give the CEO the authorisation to be the mediator? Do you agree to set a certain time to pass before going to the next step in the conflict resolution? More on the options that you have in Chapter 9.

Agreement on what happens in case of cofounder's death/incapacitation/divorce

This is a very specific scenario when a cofounder leaves and it is no longer her who would be potentially deciding on voting on the shares. Unless otherwise agreed, the shares of the business become part of the general inheritance or common matrimonial property to be split between the spouses – in this case, the remaining cofounders. The ownership right as such is defined, however, depending on what is possible in your country and for your type of company; you might add limitations on voting rights connected with the shares in such a scenario. For details do consult with a local lawyer.

Partnership Charter

For some of the 'soft' parts of your agreement, I recommend you to summarise them in the partnership charter, which you attach as an amendment to your cofounder agreement. The advantage is that if you need to change any of these agreements, you do not need to change the cofounder agreement itself so it gives more flexibility. This part is not meant to be legally binding and enforceable but provides a good basis and point of reference for the team going forward. If you would like to get more details on this topic there is a very useful book by David Gage, *The Partnership Charter*. In general, recommended topics to be covered include:

Commitment

Fleshing out the cofounders' commitment – especially relevant if not all cofounders join the business full time from the start – deals with availability (weekends in or out?), response time (if not on holidays), how much time per week/month? When is the commitment to join the business full time?

Communication

How did you agree as a team to communicate? A commitment to be open, honest, timely, and professional are some of the typical features to mention. It can also deal with the frequency (for example minimum monthly team meeting) and means (phone, physical, which tools to use).

Manifesto/mission/vision

Some cofounding teams decide to summarise what they want to achieve with the business, and based on which values, in a manifesto summarising their vision and mission. It might sound fluffy in the beginning but if you for example choose sustainability as one of your values and the next client that knocks on your door is a coal mine, nuclear power plant or genetically modified soy trader, you might save yourself a lengthy discussion on whether to take on that assignment.

Milestones and feedback

Specifying the milestones is especially important if they are linked to shares vesting and should align with your business plan and cofounders' roles. An important feature is regular performance feedback to measure the progress against your agreed milestones. Again, hopefully this is not a case within your team but should you ever have to deal with an issue of a cofounder whose performance is questionable, having both the ability to check it against the initial agreement and records on regular feedback is priceless.

Policies

This should include any other policies you agreed for working together. One example is policy on hiring family members; this could be a very minor but sensitive topic – do you foresee/allow hiring family members? If so, under which conditions, for example reporting to someone else? Another example might be commitment to gender equality and how you want to execute it.

Operations

The important aspects on operations include the outline of the cofounders' commitment, time tracking (if required), response time and availability, communication, expenses recording and reimbursement rules, and representation to third parties. This is typically part of the partnership charter as an attachment to the cofounder agreement.

Focus On Business But Your Agreement Is Not To File And Forget

The process to come to an alignment and an agreement with your cofounders, to be summarised in your cofounder agreement, is a big part of the value. All the teams I worked with facilitating this process up until now discovered some valuable insights during this process. Similarly, there is a lot of potential value in maximising the benefits the agreement gives to your partnership, by being a living helping hand to assist you, the CEO of the business, to steer the team.

Processes and checks

I know there are few things in life which sound more boring, tedious and end up on the 'will deal with it later means never' to do list. This is about increasing the success of your business though. You are of course free to skip this section, but as you have already made it thus far on the responsible and sensible cofounder path, please do not.

Your cofounder agreement covers hard legal aspects and in the partnership charter also the 'soft' parts such as commitment, how you work together and vision and expectations of the cofounding team (in the partnership charter). This is a very helpful map that you can, and hopefully will, use frequently as your business grows and you will be making important strategic decisions on the way. Whether it is on expanding your team with new employees, getting an external investment or growing your products/service offering to a new client segment for example. You will not need to draw the map every time when you reach a milestone on your journey and are set for the next phase.

Decision making and communication

If you agreed for example a minimum one-monthly team meeting, do arrange for the first few – blocking the time and defining how you do it (call? meeting?). It is important to start the right habit and make sure that you do what you agreed.

Time tracking

Did you agree on tracking the time of the team in any shape and form? If yes, how are you going to do it? Who is responsible for keeping the timesheets complete and up-to-date? Which tools will you use and what is expected from the cofounders to provide and when?

 You can find as your starter some of the time tracking tools in the resource section on cofounding.info.

Feedback

Recommended is to have at a minimum annual, ideally quarterly, feedback sessions with the team to check if all the cofounders are performing as expected, keeping their commitment and satisfyingly fulfilling their roles. As in any relationship, honest, professional and frequent communication is absolutely essential to get the best possible value from the relationship. If there are any doubts about the performance of anyone on the team it is also crucial after providing the feedback to allocate the time frame and specific requirements for correction.

 You can find a template and resources in the resource section on cofounding.info.

As the world has changed, do we need to change too?

> ## "Change is the only constant."
>
> Heraklitus

As your business grows you might realise that you have pivoted, you changed your business strategy, you changed your initial customer focus or distribution channels. Your business is simply reacting to the change happening around you all the time, which is perfectly fine. Important is that your cofounding team and agreements reflect the changes. Make it a good practice to regularly review your cofounding agreement to see if all the aspects are still appropriate and valid. For example, during the evaluation of the year, before the Christmas party. Especially for agreements that include milestones-based vesting, the regular review is a must.

Ready To Implement Your Cofounder Agreement

Once you have agreed on all the main inputs of the cofounder agreement it is time to implement it. The implementation is the easy part – it means that you prepare a written cofounder agreement, have all your cofounders sign it and implement the processes that you need to support the agreements that you made.

Do it yourself

A while ago I was participating in a variation of 'Fuck Up Night' – the honest lessons sharing where startup founders share their mistakes and the valuable lessons learned in a panel discussion. During one of the unfortunate stories of cofounder issues (by now it should not be a surprise for you that there were many), we had the following question from the audience: 'Can I just download a standard template somewhere and do it myself?' The answer was: 'Sure you can – just be aware that this is potentially one of the most important building blocks of your business, and if you do it wrong, the question is not if but when it will cost you your business.'

I would not have such a black and white opinion as the cofounder and it is clearly the pain of losing his business over a cofounding dispute that has made him quite extreme on the topic. There are good materials out there and depending how complex your cofounding team agreement is, you can use them as a starting point. I would urge you, however, to be critical of your (and your team's) skills and knowledge to evaluate whether you:

a)   Fully do it yourself.

b)   Do it yourself and ask for a professional review.

Especially when your agreement involves some type of vesting schedule (which I truly hope it does if you chose the fixed equity split), different types of shares, any deviation from standard decision making or profit allocation or different asset investment (for example pre-existing intellectual property), I would strongly advise you to have the agreement reviewed by a professional (lawyer or startup mentor). The review is a relatively economical budget option and depending on the quality of your starting draft should not command more than one to three hours. If your draft needs more time the good news is that you are not building a business on an unsolid foundation and it is still much cheaper to fix it now than later.

The chance that you will need to refer back to your initial agreement is high so this is not a part of your entrepreneurial journey to skip or do as quickly and cheaply as possible.

If you chose the dynamic equity split model, Mike Moyer and a team of dedicated Slicing Pie lawyers are working hard to make standardised templates for implementing the dynamic equity split elements available. Depending on the country, the agreement templates may be from full cofounder agreements and may contain clauses to be added to an already existing cofounder agreement. Check carefully which is the option for your country and for the stage you are in (pre-incorporation or after incorporation).

Legal contractual essentials for the DIY cofounders

This section is not meant to (and cannot) make you a legal contractual expert in two pages. I put it together based on the most common DIY contracts mistakes that I have seen, so it is a good checklist for any contract that you are drafting yourself:

- Clear identification of all parties to the agreement: for individuals, this includes full name, date of birth, address, ID number, nationality – the idea is that you need to be able to clearly and without any doubt identify who the party is.

- Clear definitions of all the terms used in the agreement: this helps to keep your agreement clearer for interpretation and enables you to use the terminology without repetitively explaining it.

- Common intention of the parties: this is typically part of the preamble of the agreement and is important when interpreting the meaning of the agreement (with the intention of the parties) in potentially unclear situations.

- Clear rules on voting rights and voting weight:

  o Decide which decision needs absolute or partial majority.

  o Decide on the cofounders' vote weight.

- Applicable law and jurisdiction: in case of dispute, what is the governing law (especially important if you have different cofounder nationalities or locations or cross-border operations) and which courts should decide (the best choice is typically to avoid any doubt and choose the court in the same place as the registered seat of the company).

Have it done for you

You can probably do pretty much everything if you set your mind on it and allocate the required resources – always a balance between where your resources are creating the most value. You can also ask a professional to do it for you.

For choosing the right advisor, do a minimal due diligence and preferably ask for recommendations. Important considerations for the advisor you choose are if you have a good personal fit (believe me), if the communication and style is aligned, if the advisor has startup experience, and last but not least having a clear pricing agreement.

Depending on your situation and complexity of the agreement, you might also need a tax expert. For the dynamic equity split choice DES is gaining a lot of popularity and relatively fast, but I cannot guarantee you that all the lawyers and tax advisors are already up to speed. To save yourself time and resources, a good start is with the dedicated Slicing Pie lawyers listed on slicingpie.com website.

Support it

The last step for implementation is to put in place the processes that will help you to implement the cofounding agreement on an ongoing basis.

For managing the dynamic equity fund a great option is to use the Slicing Pie tool on slicingpie.com. You benefit from the predefined formulas (for ongoing cofounders, new founders joining, founders exiting), different log-in interfaces (the administrator sees the setting and all the share allocations, the individual users see only their share), and an easy way for the cofounders to record their expenses and contributions.

Slicing Pie fund record [25]

Checklist

- Before company incorporation: I am covered by a written cofounder agreement with a clear definition of what is a potential future equity share and what, if any, is the potential compensation for the other parties I am working with if we do not proceed further with the project.

- After company incorporation: we have a written, signed and archived cofounder (shareholder) agreement which addresses all the main topics of the partnership: equity split, decision making, voting rights, liabilities, intellectual property assignment, anti-competition, disputes resolution and cofounders' death/incapability.

- We have a partnership charter summarising cofounders' commitment, communication guidelines, business mission/vision/purpose, milestones and feedback process, policies and operations guidelines (time tracking, expense recording).

CHAPTER 8:

CHANGES IN YOUR COFOUNDING TEAM

Change being the only constant, the question is not whether but when and what changes in your cofounding team will you deal with. In this chapter you will learn:

- The main different scenarios under which a cofounder can leave a team, typical mistakes, and what should you always have in your cofounder agreement to be prepared and safeguard your business.

- Accommodating a new cofounder joining the team.

- Accommodating other parties joining the business.

- What you need to take care of when terminating the business partnership.

Plan vs reality

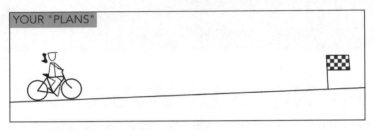

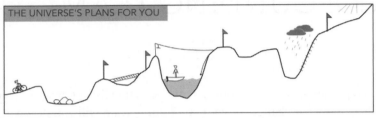

© DOGHOUSE DIARIES

Apparently, the best way to make God laugh is to tell him about your plans. Despite us often wanting it to be otherwise, change is a constant, even more so in the startup phase of a business. Some industries are more fast-moving than others, but in my experience it is not the industry which is the most determining factor of change, it is the people. It was necessary in the 'dating times' with your cofounders to understand their context to decide if and how you wanted to work together. And as useful as it is, it was a snapshot in a certain point of time. And it is not realistic to expect that it will remain unchanged for the next x years that you plan to grow the business. And there are two main factors: either the cofounders' situation changes or your business changes and the cofounder might no longer be a best fit. Or your team will expand. Being prepared for change is the smartest strategy to benefit from it when it happens. And chances are, it will.

> ## "It is not the strongest of the species that survive, not the most intelligent, but the ones most responsive to change."
>
> Charles Darwin

Cofounder Is Leaving The Team

There are many possible reasons why a cofounder might leave a team and whenever it happens it can be a very disruptive event in the early stage of a business. What is important is to be prepared that it might happen and agree upfront what will happen in such cases. And it happens more often than you will want to know. There are plenty of famous examples of cofounders being fired or leaving, with or without the businesses trying to reclaim their shares – ranging from Steve Jobs (Apple), Sandy Lerner (Cisco), Andrew Mason (Groupon), Eduardo Saverin (Facebook) – the list is endless. So whether the story is famous or not, big or small, early or later – cofounders leave. It is a fact of life.

The consequences for your business will be different depending on which stage you are at – if prior to incorporation in the simple partnership or after incorporation and the cofounder is already a shareholder in your company. A cofounder leaving the operative or management position in the business is one step. A second step is to deal with the leaving cofounder's ownership in the business – whether it is her participation in the partnership or part of the equity of the company. Depending on how amicable or adversarial the relationship with the leaving cofounder is at that stage, it will be an easier or more difficult conversation. Given all the possible variables (timing, legal context etc.), the purpose of this section is to give you an overview of the possible issues and highlight which actions are recommended to take to be as safe and ready as possible if this situation happens.

The starting point is the equity recovery framework. If you do not have one you might end up with so-called 'dead equity' – people owning part of the equity who are no longer involved with the business. It is problematic as it impacts the ownership, decision making and the amount of equity you have available for further growth – whether it is to get new cofounders on the team or for potential investors.

Other negative consequences, which are to a certain extent unavoidable but can be mitigated when discussed upfront, include:

- Delay in the business growth execution.

- Need to replace the leaving cofounder resources (time, skills, knowledge).

- Potential leakage and ownership issues regarding intellectual property or strategic know-how.

Equity recovery framework

The allocation of equity is one decision you need to make and agree on with your cofounders. Equally important is to agree on the equity recovery framework – what happens with the equity share if a cofounder leaves the business. You can consider including agreement on limited transferability of the shares as well as priority right for the company and other shareholders to buy out the equity. Important in this case is to agree what will be the buyout price. A typical agreement will go for the same price as offered by a third party, and in the absence of a third party benchmark, a pre-agreed valuation method of the company and then its proportionate part. Be aware though that, in general, business valuation, despite looking an exact science and delivering seemingly decimal point exactness, is more black box magic and very dependent on the input assumptions. The range between two experts doing the valuation for the same business can still be fairly broad and it is typically not possible to set all the variables in stone upfront. The suitable valuation method will be depending on the type of business venture and its development stage. If you are not familiar with the basics for including the methodology and framework in your cofounder agreement, ask for expert advice. If the company already has a stable cash flow, some of the traditional accounting methods use discounted cash flow, earnings multiples or discretionary cash flow. For the high-potential, high-growth startups without cash flow, some of the typical valuation methods are market comparison valuation, step-up valuation or risk mitigation valuation. A good starting point if you decide to go the learn yourself way is the *Founder's Pocket Guide: Startup valuation* by Stephen Poland.

Another useful point to consider is the distinction between different scenarios under which the cofounder could be leaving the company, whether it is voluntary (a cofounder deciding to leave) or involuntary (a cofounder being asked to leave).

Cofounder leaving general

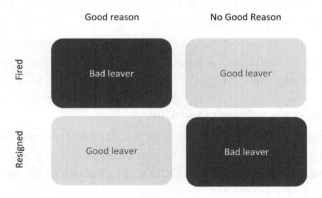

To protect both the cofounders and the business, it is helpful to include some type of good leaver/bad leaver scenarios in your recovery framework and assign different consequences for the equity ownership of the leaving cofounder. The devil being in the detail though, you need to define as exactly as you possibly can the good and bad leaver scenario and at a minimum verify what is possible for the equity consequences in your situation (timing – before or after incorporation; type of legal entity; existing legal; and tax regulation).

The good leaver by resignation

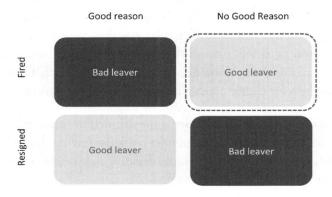

The good leaver in general is a cofounder who when leaving does not have any punitive element in the treatment of her equity. A typical situation when a cofounder resigns for good reason might include significant and unforeseen change in her personal, family or health situation or significant changes in the business that effectively push the cofounder out.

Change in the cofounder's situation

The personal situation could be that a cofounders' partner needs to relocate and it is not suitable for the business that she will stay in the team and work remotely. Or that the changed family or health situation of a cofounder significantly limits her availability for the business to a point when it makes sense that she resigns.

Change in the business situation

Some examples that could remove the cofounder's ability to keep her original commitment could be a significant change in her role or compensation (without her agreeing to that) or change in the business location.

As disruptive as it potentially could be for the business, there is not much that the leaving cofounder can or could have done to prevent this situation and therefore she should keep the reward – the full equity already allocated.

 Joan and Maria started a cosmetics studio together, with Joan being a slight majority owner with 60% of the equity and Maria having 40% of the equity. After the first three years when the business was stable and profitable, Maria had a child who was born handicapped and required special care. Her commitment and availability to the business significantly changed. On the other hand, Joan had started to develop her own cosmetic products line and had plans to expand the business and potentially create a franchise. They both agreed that it did not make sense for Maria to remain a cofounder and settled on her exiting the business, with Joan buying her existing equity stake for a fair market price.

The good leaver by termination

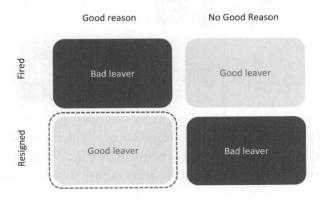

Another possible scenario is that the cofounder is fired by the company for no good reason. The cofounder was performing her role well. It could be the change of ownership or change of strategy of the majority decision maker in the team who decides that the cofounder is no longer wanted in the team. In such a case, the cofounder should also be protected and keep the full equity already allocated.

You might still want to include an agreement that if such a situation happens, the business can offer the leaving good leaver cofounder to buy out her equity for a fair market price, to avoid the dead equity issue. In the good leaver situation – whether resignation or termination – the cofounder should be protected for the investment that she made in the business. The equity she owns at the point in time when she leaves the company should either be bought out for fair market price or she should be allowed to keep it.

The bad leaver by resignation

On the opposite end of the scale, in the bad leaver scenario the cofounder either leaves the business for no good reason or is fired for a good reason.

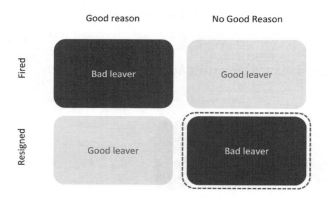

An example of resignation for no good reason is that the cofounder received a more attractive offer elsewhere. Another example is that the cofounder lost interest or motivation in the business. Whichever of these situations apply, the cofounder leaving because of the lack of commitment and/or loyalty can be very disruptive for your business. You might need to find a new cofounder with similar capabilities, get her up to speed and allocate new equity for the new cofounder to join the team.

 Jacqueline, Hugo and Greg started a strategy consulting company focused on a niche market of business angels' investors. The idea was to combine their specific skill sets and create an offer which was unique in the market. At that time, the business angels could find each of the expertises separately, but the new value created by their idea was to combine it, which was validated by initial market testing. The starting agreement of the cofounders was that Jacqueline would be the first cofounder to work for the business full-time and in the period of six months, when there would be more secured future revenue, Hugo and Greg would join as well.

In the meantime, Hugo got a very interesting offer to become a European head of strategy for an American company expanding in Europe. The financial rewards short term – both the amount and the security – were so attractive for Hugo that he decided to leave the cofounding team. Because of Hugo leaving the team, the business suffered. The ongoing projects already agreed with the clients got delayed, as Jacqueline and Greg had to find someone else who could provide Hugo's expertise. Hugo's decision to choose the offer that was personally more attractive to him therefore did damage the investment that Jacqueline and Greg put into the business. As opposed to the good leaver situation, Hugo could have decided otherwise and stayed with the team to honour his original commitment. In this situation, it is only fair that there will be some negative impact on the reward he is entitled to for his investment in the business.

The bad leaver by termination

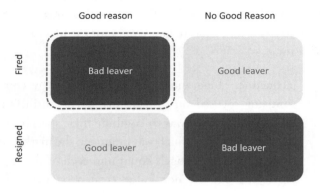

Another variation of bad leaver is when the cofounder is fired for a good reason. Typically, these situations involve the cofounder's behaviour and/or non-performance. For the performance-related issues, this confirms the absolute necessity to have defined performance, commitment and delivery expectations when you start working together. Evaluating performance as good or bad, sufficient or not sufficient is only fairly possible against agreed and clear expectations. Anyone in such a situation should also have a chance to first receive warning that will enable her to correct the situation. Only after the warning and having reasonable chance and time to correct the situation and not correcting it is it fair to fire a cofounder for a good reason.

Similarly, as in the other bad leaver situation, it is only fair to have negative consequences on the reward for the slacking cofounder. For the behaviour-related issues – typically including damaging the business, stealing, sexual harassment, unethical or illegal behaviour – it is also recommended to have the mutual and explicit agreement of the team that the consequence of such behaviour would be to fire any cofounder who would do it.

Michael, Thomas and Lucas joined forces to start an online art trading platform. Lucas was invited to join the team for the technical/programming expertise that he would bring to develop the first prototype. After a few months and several unpleasant discussions, Michael and Thomas unfortunately had to conclude that Lucas was not delivering. It was partially due to his low commitment, combined with lack of the programming skills, to finalise the prototype. As they had agreed to use the dynamic equity split based on the Slicing Pie method they applied the recovery framework included. By that time the only contribution that Lucas brought to the business was his time. As Lucas was fired for non-performance (and it was possible as the team had upfront clearly defined what was Lucas' role), he was not entitled to any equity in the business.

Different equity consequences for good and bad leaver scenario

The Slicing Pie dynamic equity split

The Slicing Pie method provides a logical and simple recovery framework. It differentiates between a good and a bad leaver, defines the main situations when the cofounder is a good or a bad leaver and does imply different consequences for being a good or a bad leaver for the equity of the leaving cofounder.

To prevent 'light' walkaway decisions and to motivate the cofounders to resolve their issues and stick around, the DES recovery framework has a punitive element for the bad leaver: his leaving equity stake is calculated without any non-cash contributions to the business. It might sound very strict, but the decision to leave without a good reason or not to perform is one that is potentially damaging the investment of all the other cofounders and the business and one that you really want to do your best to prevent.

On the other side of the coin, life happens and if the cofounder has to leave the business (serious personal or health reasons for example) or is fired for no good reason (greedy and unfair founders with majority voting rights do exist), the cofounder who invested his resources into the business is protected and keeps his equity stake, with the company having an option to buy him out for a fair price.

Fixed equity splits recovery framework

For businesses that do fixed equity splits, the best way to be prepared for the leaving cofounder situation is to include some dynamic component, preferably vesting with a cliff. Within the common one-year cliff period, you should be able to determine sufficiently if the cofounder on the team is a good fit for the business and is delivering sufficient performance. If you do implement this arrangement, it gives you a similar option as a probation period with employees. However, in any type of scenario you want to be fair, which includes addressing any underperformance issues early with a sufficient time to correct or, whilst protecting your equity, still giving a leaving cofounder some compensation for the work they did deliver even if they leave within the cliff period.

Cofounders prior to incorporation of legal entity

This is potentially the most challenging category as many cofounders are not aware that they created a partnership and what the consequences are. The best advice is to have the discussion as soon as you start working together with someone, clearly outlining the framework for the cooperation in your cofounder agreement – whether it is a test period, what happens if you continue working together and what happens if not and whether there is right to any compensation if the project does not go further. The local legal regulations are decisive here on what is possible, as in some cases partners leaving a simple partnership means automatic termination of the partnership.

Implementation of the equity recovery framework

The decision on what are the consequences and scenarios of a cofounder leaving should be defined in advance in the cofounder agreement. Whether it is on amicable terms or not, a cofounder leaving a business is very often an emotional and potentially tense situation. Crucial aspects of your business, including intellectual property or equity ownership, should not be left to decide on at the worst possible time, which in this case is when the cofounder is leaving.

As much as I recommend including some type of good/bad leaver arrangement in your cofounding agreement, you should know about the typical challenges of this type of arrangement.

Firstly, especially when there are different consequences on the leaving cofounder equity stake, the classification whether the leaving cofounder is a good leaver or bad leaver is logically a very sensitive one. And chances are that the cofounder who is leaving might have a different opinion from the rest of the team. What happens if in that specific situation it is not clear whether it falls in the good or bad leaver category? Will that be decided by vote? And what if there are only two cofounders? It is important to define the good and bad leaver terms as simply and as clearly as possible. In some countries, the legal regulations (commercial law or employment law) have similar situations defined. If so, you might need to use the existing regulation and case law as a guidance.

The second frequent problem is to establish the fair market price. I would love to tell you the one magical formula, but the fact is that there is none. Especially in the early stage of the business, the opinions on how to value the business vary widely. It also happens frequently that in case of disagreement, both parties hire valuation experts who come with very different valuation results. A good proxy for fair market value is what an independent party would offer for the business (or stake in the business). But an external benchmark is not always available. If you can – and this depends on the type of business you are starting – define the valuation framework and main assumptions to be used in such a scenario.

Most importantly, this is one of the discussions you really want to have as a team at the beginning of your cooperation. It is much easier for the teams to deal with a leaving cofounder when everyone involved knew upfront that it can happen and what are the consequences when it happens. The disruption to your business is not possible to fully mitigate, but if you have the recovery framework defined and agreed, it will help you with lowering the risk or extent of the dead equity and valuation questions leading to lengthy discussions and potentially even lawsuits.

Another important aspect when a cofounder leaves a team is to summarise the terms and conditions in a separation agreement with the leaving cofounder, covering the intellectual property ownership, anti-competition clauses and, if applicable, the shares transfer and the shares repurchase price, as well as potential confidentiality and no future claims agreement.

New Cofounder Joins The Team

Or the opposite will happen. Your original cofounders all stay and you decide to grow the cofounding team and add a new cofounder. This could happen for example if there is a need for additional resource (time, skills, expertise, network etc.) to continue and adding a cofounder is the best way to fulfil that need. Again, please do the same considerations as you did in the beginning for your cofounding team. From evaluating if adding a cofounder is the best possible way to get the resource, to selecting the right cofounder, to getting to know her/him and ensuring the alignment with the business. The same as for the original team composition applies; with every new cofounder, the complexity of the team increases exponentially, so do it right.

It is also important to discuss with the original cofounding team the basic framework for adding a new cofounder:

- Who decides and how will the decision be taken – do you want all cofounders to agree? Majority? Only the CEO?

- Who would you consider as an additional cofounder – what qualifications or qualities? Values? Expectations?

The role of the new cofounder needs to be as clear and carefully defined as for the others and the team needs to be committed to welcome the new cofounder – and also go with her through the forming, storming, norming and performing stage. Adding an additional member is very likely to have an impact on the team dynamics, requiring the team to go through the same process again.

Fixed equity splits

With adding any new cofounder to the team, you need to decide what equity stake will the new cofounder get? Is there a buy-in payment? What will be the vesting period? From where will the new equity stake come? Proportionately diluting all the existing cofounders?

Dynamic equity split solution

For the Slicing Pie dynamic equity businesses, the good news is the flexibility of the arrangement as the new cofounder is simply added to the fund. Any input that she brings will be added to the pie and she starts to 'earn' her slices as she starts working with the business, in the same way as the other cofounders. Just because it is easy though does not mean you should do it without deciding that it is the best way. One of my clients had at one point over 40 'cofounders' participating in the pie fund. Besides having difficulties in managing a team of 40 'cofounders', the number itself indicated the inexperience of the business and discouraged any potential investors to invest in the company.

Other Parties Join The Business

In the early stages, the typical other parties joining the business are investors or early employees.

Similarly to the other scenarios, it is very valuable to have the conversation with your cofounding team – upfront – about how and when you want other parties to join the business. What requirements would you have for an investor? Financial only or would you also be looking for an alignment with the business values? What type of people do you want to hire? The early stage employees are – similar to cofounders – having a significant influence on developing the business culture. You want to decide from the beginning if you want to reserve an equity pool for other parties potentially joining your business in the future.

There are no right or wrong answers to these questions, nor are there universal formulas to apply. The right answers to these questions are very much dependent on the context of your business and your team values and motivation. For the teams with a predominant control driver the tendency is to delay inviting third parties as late as possible to maintain majority of the control. For teams with a predominant profit driver the opposite applies. The sooner the business gets financing, the faster it can grow and scale, so their time framework for getting investors on board will be very different. What matters is to think about this and discuss it with your team.

 Marta, Leon and Stephan developed a healthy urban takeaway lunch concept. The success of the first location they opened was so obvious that they received the first investment offers to scale the concept only five months after starting the business. While Marta and Leon wanted to accept and grow the business as fast as possible, Stephan preferred to maintain the control and grow the business more slowly and organically, being convinced that having external investors so early would create a risk of losing the success of the concept before it was sufficiently defined and stable.

As Stephan held a majority of the equity and decision power his decision was the final one and the investment offer was not accepted. The disagreement caused Marta and Leon to lose motivation in the business and ultimately leave. Stephan was not able to find replacements for his two initial cofounders quickly enough and even the first initially successful location had to be closed. Had the founders talked about their motivation and this scenario upfront perhaps they would have decided not to start the business together as the gap was too wide. Or they would have found an acceptable compromise earlier – when the concrete offer was not on the table and the emotions were not as high.

Terminating The Business Partnership

When terminating the business partnership there are always consequences to deal with. Before all the partners can go separate ways, the business needs to be settled and the books closed.

It includes a decision on how to deal with any existing liabilities or profit. For business partnerships in the form of a limited liability company the liabilities are typically limited to the required capital input set by law and any profits or liabilities are split based on the equity shares. For simple partnerships – the ones you might have unknowingly entered when starting to work with someone – the partners' liability is joint and unlimited. This means that if one or more of the cofounders are not able to meet their liability share within the partnership, the other partners become responsible for that share of the liability.

Chris and Lucas were working for a few months on developing a social platform to enable people to meet new friends based on their hobbies and values. Unfortunately they did not get to the product market fit confirmation and decided to abort the mission. However, at that time they spent a few thousand on the technical prototype of the platform. They initially agreed that they would split the costs. When the project was being terminated, Lucas did not have the funds to pay his part of the development costs and Chris learned the bitter lesson of the joint liability by having to pay it all by himself. As they had the simple partnership – where the liability is joint and unlimited – Chris did not have any other option than to cover the cost. Had they had a cofounder agreement, Chris would have had a solid claim for his part of the costs. Moreover, if he were aware of the liability – and his exposure – he might not have allowed the cost to reach the final amount.

Other questions include who will be executing the liquidation? What will happen with any existing assets that could potentially have value? How will the business be valued? If there are any continuing activities, who will be entitled to keep using the business name and who will get the existing customers? Will there be an impact on the personal side? How will you want to deal with that?

Thinking about this scenario does not mean that you do not believe in the business to start with! It is similar to the prenuptial agreements before getting married. You do not want this option to happen, but if it does, you do want to deal with it the best way you can. And that often means agreeing some basic rules of the game upfront.

Checklist

- We discussed with the team what happens if a cofounder leaves.

- We considered some type of good/bad leaver clause.

- We discussed under which circumstances would the team consider adding new parties? Cofounders? Investors? Employees?

CHAPTER 9:

THERE IS TROUBLE IN PARADISE

> **"All wars are follies, very expensive and very mischievous ones. In my opinion, there never was a good war or a bad peace."**
>
> Benjamin Franklin

In the spirit of hope for the best while being prepared for the worst, it is unrealistic to expect that during your business partnership your team will not encounter disagreements and conflict. And it is not a bad thing! It brings an opportunity to surface underlying tension, improve understanding and self-knowledge and, if done well, actually increase the team's cohesion.

Depending on how serious the disagreement is, it is good to know which options you have to resolve conflicts and what is your team's preference on conflict resolution when it occurs.

Conflicts are typically not a pleasant experience and depending on the maturity and awareness of the participants, they can lead to very different outcomes. One possible outcome could be a renewed sense of purpose and motivation and better team performance. The other, depending on the nature of the conflict, is slow or quick deterioration of the team, possibly leading to an end of it. The choice is yours and depends a lot on how you prepare your team for the possibility of the conflict before it happens as well as how you deal with the conflict when it happens. As much as easy paths typically do not lead to interesting locations, conflicts, however unpleasant, do offer an opportunity for your cofounding team to emerge stronger out of them.

There Are A Few Conflict Resolution Options

The full range is from internal negotiation to external litigation. And they differ in many things, mainly:

- Your involvement as opposed to involvement of other parties.

- Amicable versus adversarial – are you resolving the conflict together as a team or are you standing on opposite sides blaming each other?

- Required resources – time, energy, money.

- The ability of the team to continue working together after the conflict is resolved.

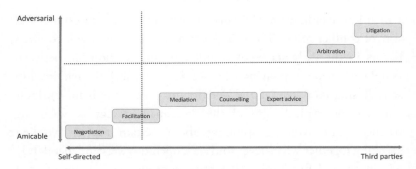

Conflict resolution options

Do It Yourself

Prevention

Not surprisingly, the best conflict resolution is to do your best to prevent conflict. Here we go back to the essential ingredients for a functioning and performing partnership: respect, trust and communication. They must be applied regularly and consistently. If at any moment you notice that there is a sensitive issue you would rather not talk through with your cofounder(s), you might be seeding a future conflict. Openly communicating about it in a respectful way, before it possibly escalates, really is the easiest option in the long run. If at any point in time you notice the open communication deteriorating, it is a red flag to be addressed. Because then you are starting to lose on one of the main benefits of partnership – the combined brain power – but also creating an environment where conflict is more likely to occur and grow. And yes, focusing on prevention can get you very far. But it is not a 100% insurance. It is the first line of defence.

Avoidance

I mention avoidance not because it is in any way a recommended way of conflict resolution. It is not. I mention it because it so often occurs in the early stages of conflict. In any relationship between people, when we stop saying what we think and feel, the relationship starts losing its potential and deteriorates. The same is for business partnerships; typical signs of the avoidance strategy is when the partners start avoiding speaking about certain topics, avoiding speaking together whatsoever, and start operating very independently within their defined roles. Potential signs of conflict are often a cofounder's slacking or overworking. The avoidance strategy seeks to defer the conflict resolution indefinitely or at least into the future. With this strategy there is a hope that the conflict will go away by itself without the confrontation. As widespread as this belief is, it almost never does. And be aware that it will get you and your team only so far. Depending on your business and how it is run, you might be able to carry on for a few weeks or months, but ultimately there will be a point when it is not possible to go any further. And more likely than not, dealing with the issue after the team grows apart is more difficult than addressing it from the start.

Negotiation

Always, always, always – make sure that you first tried your utmost to resolve the conflict internally within the team. There are some ground rules that can help you and your team and it is one of the aspects I would strongly recommend to outline in your partnership charter upfront. When the emotions are stirred it is useful to have a reference point to remind all of you how you agreed to resolve the conflict. The internal negotiation is the most cooperative and amicable way. Next to the advantage of having the lowest costs (no fees to external parties), it is also the one that has the highest chance to succeed (as everyone in your team is personally invested in the solution you all agree to) and guarantees least damage to the relationship.

Internal conflict resolution ground rules:

1. Choose a facilitator for the negotiation within the team.

2. Agree on the process.

3. Treat everyone with respect.

4. Make sure that everyone can remain calm – separate the emotion from the issue – if needed take the time out until everyone is calm enough to continue.

5. Start with the big picture – reminding the team on your joint purpose and why it is in everyone's interest to resolve the conflict.

6. Outline communication rules – one of the successful strategies recommended by communication specialists is that each party has a limited amount of time (e.g. three minutes) to voice their opinion without anyone being allowed to interrupt. This is beneficial as everyone gets the chance to be heard *and* because of the set structure it typically results in better listening as the others are not busy thinking about when to interrupt and how to respond to the points they do not agree with.

7. Identify the problem and when doing so look beyond the immediate conflict. A very useful framework to use for the discussion can be provided by the following questions:

    o What is your concern? (e.g. what does this person defend/protect and why?)

    o What is your ideal solution/arrival point? (What is that person aiming at?)

    o What do you/we need now?

8. Ask each cofounder what they wish for and evaluate if there is sufficient common ground to resolve the conflict and reach the agreement.

9. If yes: a) Ensure everyone's commitment to the solution and b) Decide what did you as a team learn out of the conflict and if there is anything you would like to implement going forward.

10. If you did not reach a satisfactory solution – ask for help.

When you did try your best and you did not achieve a solution, ask for help. Asking for help in that situation is a sign of sound judgment and strength. There is no point in keep throwing the spaghetti at the wall!

Asking For Help

The other options for conflict resolution are involving third parties to help you. The choices you have will depend on what you agreed in your partnership agreement and what is the most suitable option for the conflict at hand. If chosen well, it can have additional beneficial side effects: you might learn more about the team, improve communication and ways of working and perhaps even get some useful tips for the future. Keep the opportunity mindset!

Facilitation

Facilitation is the closest method to internal negotiation, with the difference being that you ask an external third party to be the facilitator. The ground rules from the negotiation section are applicable and effective in the same way. The more respected the external facilitator is by the team, the higher benefit there is to have the external facilitator to lead the process. The facilitator is typically (unlike with the internal option) only involved in the facilitation process. In the internal negotiation the facilitator has a double role to facilitate the process and also participate as a cofounder. In the case of an external facilitator, the person does not get involved with the content of the conflict; she focuses instead on helping the cofounders with the process and to find the common ground. Costs are relatively limited to the reward of the external facilitator. Similar to the internal negotiations, for this option to be worth trying you need the commitment and willingness of the team to resolve the conflict. If any of the parties already 'checked out' or is not able to remain calm, the facilitation is unlikely to lead to a resolution of the conflict.

Expert advice

> **"Advice is seldom welcome – those who need it the most like it the least."**
>
> Chesterfield

This option is inviting a third party to actively help to find a solution by providing an expert advice recommendation. The typical experts to involve are lawyers, accountants or business consultants, potentially already working closely with the business and being trusted advisors. They examine the conflict and after listening to all parties provide their expert recommendations.

You do need the commitment of the whole team to use this method and even more importantly the independent status of the expert. If any cofounder might believe that the expert has a closer relationship to any other cofounder that could result in biased advice, it is a waste of time to try this option. Even if you have these two, the expert advice option is unfortunately often not very successful. The main reason is that it is an advice from an external party without having the authority to impose it. To paraphrase Carl Jung: 'Good advice will never hurt anyone since nobody ever follows it.'

Depending on the complexity of the issue at hand, the expert (unlike the facilitator) needs time to examine the content of the issue as she is providing advice on the content, not the process. The costs include the expert's fee.

Counselling

Counselling could work well for specific conflict situations, as it addresses interpersonal issues as opposed to underlying business issues. The success of this option is dependent on the experience and skills of the chosen counsellor and on the commitment of the involved cofounders to participate. The counsellor focuses on the dysfunctionality in the communication and underlying relationship, helping the parties to find a way to start communicating effectively so they can continue and resolve the underlying business issue themselves. This option might require a longer time as interpersonal issues are typically not a one-session fix, and costs include the fee of the counsellor. If you do have the buy-in of the parties and a trusted counsellor for a long term, it is still one of the amicable options that can actually improve – instead of harm – the cofounders' team relationships.

Mediation

Mediation is the full involvement third party option. The mediator or mediators get fully involved with the process and with the issue itself. Important prerequisites are again the full commitment of the cofounders to resolve the issue as mediation is not binding. They need to recognise that they are in the conflict together and that it is in their best interests to resolve the conflict. The mediator, similar to a third party facilitator or a business expert, must be perceived by the parties as neutral. A mediator's job is to help the cofounders with the process as well as helping them to find a solution. Experienced mediators involve in the mediation anyone who has a stake in the conflict and might be helpful in its resolution. They create an environment for constructive dialogue and get the buy-in of all cofounders to implement the solution. They encourage the parties to talk together and are allowed to – and often do – talk to the parties separately or in smaller groups. A mediator controls the process and facilitates the solution but it is the cofounders that control the outcome. Unlike arbitration or litigation, mediation is not binding and implementation of the solution is voluntary. Without the commitment of the cofounders to the mediation it is unlikely to work and therefore might not be worth the time and cost. Costs are the mediator's fee. It is not advisable to involve other third parties, such as lawyers, in the mediation process.

Arbitration

Arbitration already belongs to the adversarial spectrum of the options. The third party invited to solve the conflict – one or more arbitrators – are controlling both the process and the outcome. They take the decision out of the cofounders' hands and the arbitration decision is binding.

Arbitration is a form of alternative dispute resolution – a conflict solution outside of the courts. The parties to the conflict agree to refer the conflict to a third party (one or more arbitrators) and agree to be bound by their resolution. An arbitration decision is typically enforceable in the court. During the arbitration process, the arbiter reviews the evidence and bases the decision on laws and legal precedents. Very often, expert witnesses and lawyers are present during the arbitration process.

Arbitration was initially invented as an alternative to the adversarial, lengthy and expensive judicial litigation. However, it developed in a somewhat similar way, being relatively adversarial, and depending on the case and arbitrators used, costly. The advantage of arbitration compared to litigation remains a relatively shorter timeline and the fact that it is private. Typically, the involved parties' relationship is damaged as the process often involves parties blaming each other, lawyers encouraging parties not to talk to each other and an imposed third party decision which inevitably creates winners and losers.

The rules of the process are often defined by the chosen arbitration association. Good practice is to decide which arbitration association you want to use and whether you prefer arbitration by one or more arbiters.

 For typical arbitration clauses check the website resources section on cofounding.info

Litigation

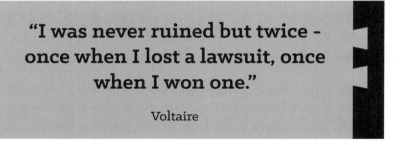

> "I was never ruined but twice - once when I lost a lawsuit, once when I won one."
>
> Voltaire

Litigation is the option of last resort. It is when there is nothing else left to do. And remember before you decide for this option even a bad agreement is better than a good lawsuit. Because litigation – similar to arbitration – is adversarial. And in public. It is a war. And wars always leave casualties on both sides.

It is going to the public courts to resolve your conflict. It is adversarial, expensive and damaging to the relationship. Depending on in which country you live and how effective and efficient the judicial system, it might be more or less lengthy. But as it typically includes a few options to appeal the court decision, the lengthy characteristics are more likely than not. If you decide to solve your conflict by litigation, be prepared to go deep into your pockets, reserve a lot of time and energy and do not think that the relationship will survive it without serious damage. On top of that, depending on the complexity of the conflict in the business context, it is also dependent on the quality of the judicial system, a bet if the judge deciding will actually understand the underlying issue. Similar to arbitration, the adversarial character of the process does create winners and losers.

Implementation

Think about it as a mixture of prevention and insurance. The preferred way to resolve conflict to be discussed with your team upfront and included in your cofounder agreement is a step-wise approach and ground rules for conflict resolution (such as the ones recommended for internal negotiation and facilitation).

The step-wise approach can choose the different options to be tried sequentially – from negotiation to mediation. For the adversarial methods, for arbitration you might want to include some procedural decision (one or more arbiters) and for litigation, choose the court jurisdiction.

All the years in business made me a firm believer that there are no win-lose solutions. Unless you find a win-win solution, it is a lose-lose solution. There might be a temporary time delay making it look like a win-lose solution, but even though you might have won the arbitration or litigation it is likely still to be a loss for everyone involved as your cofounding team will look different afterwards.

Conflicts are usually in one of these three categories:

a) Personal or relationship: typically, they relate to conflicting communication styles, loss of trust, disrespect, or breach of confidence. These typically involve one cofounder believing that she is more important or valuable to the partnership than the others, unclear management agreements leading to overlapping roles, or no one being clearly responsible for a specific task.

   Suitable conflict resolution for personal or relationship issues is facilitation, counselling or mediation.

b) Business issue: these conflicts are evolving around goals, procedures and processes – they are fairly tangible and concrete. Typical examples are cofounders' commitment and performance or equity ownership. However, underneath are often misalignments in the bigger picture – on the purpose and vision of the business – so make sure that you dig deeper when identifying the conflict.

   Suitable conflict resolution could be expert advice, facilitation or mediation.

c) Conflict of interest: your team might encounter these conflicts when there is a misalignment in the context – whether it is the profit versus control driver, or the fit of the business in the cofounder life (imagine one cofounder wants to retire therefore is in favour of accepting the buyout offer, the other wants to continue and grow the business further).

   Suitable conflict resolution could be expert advice, facilitation or mediation.

The golden trio of conflict resolution

The most important tools to help you to deal with any conflict are:

1. Have the rules on how you want to deal with the conflict when it occurs.

2. Address the conflict as soon as you see it happening.

3. Always, always remember that the best solution is an immediate win-win solution.

 ## Checklist

- We discussed how we want to resolve conflicts.

- We decided a step-based approach and described it in our cofounder agreement.

- We outlined guidelines for internal communication and negotiation in our partnership charter.

CHAPTER 10:

DONE WRONG? HERE IS HOW YOU FIX IT

Is it better to get everything right from the start? Of course! It is easier, quicker and cheaper. But every now and then you might find yourself living in a less than ideal world and realise that if you knew some things about your current business partnership you would have done it differently. It is OK and corrective action now is better than no corrective action at all. It is not fatal to make a mistake, but it might be fatal to ignore it instead of fixing it.

And yes, I would hope for you that you have a cofounding agreement in place which deals with some of the major aspects for cofounders' commitment, performance, roles, equity allocation framework and equity recovery framework. Because dealing with any of the situations outlined below is much easier by simply referring to the agreement you made.

If not, do not panic. Do identify which one of the categories your current hindrance falls into. Depending how solid and documented your initial agreements were, you will have easier or more difficult ways to solve the situation. Fairness to all involved, a sensitive and sensible approach and addressing the issue as soon as you identified it are the best mitigating factors.

The Typical Pains

You are in a business partnership and you realised it is not for you

After some time working together, you realised that the partnership was not the right choice. You skipped step 1. It could be because as you built the business you realised that you have all the essential resources to get the business going by yourself. Or you would prefer to keep the full control of the business and decide by yourself. Or you are not a team player. Either way you would prefer to reclaim the full control and ownership of the business. It is fair to admit this to yourself and to your cofounders. Because continuing in a business partnership while you would rather do it by yourself is unlikely to be a successful and fulfilling experience for anyone involved. At the same time, it is only fair to appreciate the investment your cofounders brought to the business until now and to treat them fairly. The best possible solution is to offer your current cofounders a buy-out.

Buy-out offer

The buy-out offer would be based on the cofounders' share of the current value of the business. Especially in the early stages, this is the sticky point. Did you agree any valuation methods in your cofounder agreement for cases when a cofounder leaves? If not, you can decide to choose a valuation expert with experience in your industry and for the business phase you are in (early stage) and jointly agree that external valuation will be used as the basis for the buy-out offer. In the end, finding a good and fair way how to buy out the cofounders in this situation is a win-win for everyone. There are different options on how to structure the buy-out payment depending on the business financial situation: it can be a one-time lump-sum payment or partial payment with a payment schedule, potentially even tying it to the future business revenues.

You have cofounders who are not fitting the business

In your cofounders' team, there are cofounders who are not fitting the business – failure in step 2. It can be because of an initial mistake when preselecting and choosing them. Or because the business strategy changed and their respective skill-set became obsolete. Whatever the reason, the best for the business and for the not-fitting cofounders is to find a way for them to exit. As in the previous scenario, the solution must be fair. Whether it was your mistake in the recruitment or a fact of business life, the not-fitting cofounder should be entitled to her share of reward for the resources they have invested.

For the buy-out offer, check the previous buy-out offer section.

You have cofounders who do not have the resources you expected

After a while working together, you realise that a cofounder does not have the resources which were the basis for accepting her to the team. Do you remember the example of Michael, Thomas and Lucas with their online art platform project? And Lucas, the CTO IT programmer who after a few months still had not delivered the prototype? In such a case this is an individual non-performance. Another scenario could be that a cofounder committed to invest a cash amount which did not happen. Whichever equity split you agreed to, the fair solution includes some punitive aspect for the non-performing or non-delivering cofounder equity. And you want to address it as soon as you notice it! Unless you have a clear recovery framework with clear performance requirements agreed, this could be an unpleasant discussion. Prepare for it by collecting all evidence on what you did agree (emails, meeting notes, other cofounder recollections) and address it as soon as you can. Hopefully your non-performing or non-delivering cofounder will appreciate and recognise the shortcoming and you can find a fair way to compensate her for part of the investment and agree on the cofounder's exit from the team – with application of the intellectual property rights assignment if applicable and the non-competition and confidentiality limitations.

Your team is not performing

This is a relatively broad diagnosis which can have different causes. The most typical are:

Roles and responsibilities misfit

Either you keep on bumping into each other and fighting over who should be responsible for taking a decision – there are too many candidates – or there are areas which are falling through the cracks as no one is taking care of them. In either case, do review the roles and responsibilities of the cofounders. Because either they are too abstract and overlapping or they are not covering all the business areas that need to be taken care of by the cofounding team. If so, (re)do the RACI exercise – Chapter 5 Getting Serious.

Working together

You have all the right resources, but somehow it does not work. You spend most of the time smoothing the edges between the cofounders. The assumption that the team would make better decisions is not holding, as either the cofounders are not contributing or many of the contributions are the same. There is lack of respect or open communication within the team. Depending on what the issue is and how serious it is, you can either try to fix it yourself (which is a good option to start with in any case) or involve an external coach to help your team. It can also be a part of the storming process that will ultimately lead to the desired performance. Or it can be a show stopper where you will need to adjust the cofounding team. It is fair for all to try hard to resolve first themselves and then to get external help before giving up. Some type of storming phase is an inevitable dynamic in any relationship! It should though just be temporary and lead to the performance phase.

Individual cofounder performance

As with sometimes hiring an employee who subsequently underperforms, this can also happen with your cofounder. Having clear expectations and role responsibilities helps to evaluate and diagnose any issues. Dealing with the issue as soon as you suspect it is happening is another mitigating factor. The underperforming cofounder should have a chance to correct it. Clear and specific communication on the underperformance is essential, together with a clear indication of the time frame for correction and how the cofounder is expected to achieve it. If the cofounder does not correct the performance within the set framework, it is time for an exit discussion.

Hopefully you do have an equity recovery framework (good/bad leaver) in place. If not, you will need to rely on your leadership skills and fairness of your cofounder to find a solution for her to exit. Fairness again can go a long way, for example to not disregard if there was a value delivered which can be used by the business. In a worst case scenario, you might need to come up with a buy-out offer for whatever equity stake the cofounder has in the business. It sucks, but the sooner you do it, the better. Delayed action can negatively affect the whole business; resentment, disagreement, even open hostility all contribute to hindering your business gaining value. Or if you can mitigate those and your business keeps growing, the buy-out value for the non-performing cofounder will be more in the future. Either way, it might be an interesting deal for the non-performing cofounder to stay as long as possible, but very unlikely to be in the best interests of your business.

Your equity split is not correct

One of the most frequent and unfortunately most difficult to correct mistakes is incorrect equity splits. Again, all is not lost, success depends a lot on how you approach it and the fairness of your fellow cofounders.

Equity split not done

In many cases the partners start to work together without agreeing on the equity split. How to best deal with this situation depends whether you did have an oral agreement, whether the other partner(s) had fixed an assumption on what would be their share, and how late in the process you are, i.e. how much investment from the cofounders into the project has already been made. On one hand, especially if the initial assumptions proved to be not correct, it is an easier process than to renegotiate a fixed and finalised equity split. That does not change the sensitivity of the situation and potential damage to the relationship, so handle with care.

Retrofit

Based on the fairness principle, a good start is to use the retrofit tool developed by Mike Moyer on slicingpie.com to estimate how the equity share would be allocated if the business used the dynamic equity split from the beginning. You do need to go back and try to recreate/ remember everything that everyone contributed since the beginning of working together. This is not an easy exercise but will provide you a good basis for the late adjustment. Because of the transparency and fairness of the method, the cofounders who are likely to have an issue with this approach are the ones who do somewhat prefer to benefit on the account of others.

Split not accurate – too early – wrong assumptions

You do have a fixed equity split agreement in place and you realise that the initial assumptions on which it was done are not correct. Do not start tearing hairs from your head, this happens more often than not! But it is not a good basis. This is a great test of your team and your leadership. And do not expect the discussions to be pleasant. Recommended is to have all involved agree on the incorrectness of the initial split and agreeing to an adjustment.

A good start can be the recalibration tool developed for the dynamic equity split by Mike Moyer on slicingpie.com. The recalibration tool simply takes the initial split and compares it to what the split would be if the equity share was determined by the dynamic equity split, based on delivered contributions of the individual cofounders. The first step is to get buy-in of the team to use this method (and agree on the input parameters). The second is to consult a lawyer and tax advisor, depending on your specific situation, on what is the best way to correct it. Most of the time, redistributing the shares between the cofounders is a better solution than issuing new shares, but you do want to understand the options and their consequences before you decide which one to implement.

You do not have a solid partnership agreement

Step 7 – after reading this book, you realised you have either no or an incomplete cofounder agreement, and you realised that now, without being in a conflicting situation with any of your cofounders. Congratulations – this is called a fix just in time. The recommendation is to sit with your team and go through steps 4, 5 and 6 and complete the missing parts of your cofounder agreement or make one (in case you did not have anything). Now you understand why it is so important to have one and can also explain to your team that it is in the interest of everyone to have it, so it is just going back a few steps to do what was not done before.

Maximise Your Chances To Fix It

Many of the discussions that you will need to have with your team are in the sensitive category. We are all typically rather resistant to change. Especially in case of the adjustments to equity splits, it is part of our psychology that it is somewhat easier for us to work for the future dangling carrot (and be relatively happy with that) than to have that carrot (or part of it) taken away from us (even though we might know that we did not deserve it). Whether you will be able to reach an agreement to get out of the situation when your cofounder team is missing some part of the solid foundation depends a lot on your skills, fairness of all involved and on what the situation is. In a worst case scenario, you might need to terminate the current project and start again on a solid base.

The advantage of an independent expert helping you

If you are an expert in any field, you do know how valuable expertise and experience is. The same counts for business partnership problems. Depending on which situation you are in, it might be the best bet – after getting the buy-in of the team to correct whatever is not right – to ask an independent expert to help you. It typically also takes some of the sensitivity out of the discussion if it is facilitated by a third party. Another benefit is that an experienced expert will help you to address all the related issues without you forgetting to include something in the correction.

For the team dynamics and working together the review of an experienced coach can be all that is needed.

For the equity split discussions the review of a business expert can help you to get the point across and facilitate the recalibration or retrofit solution.

When you need to come up with a buy-out offer for a cofounder, similarly helpful can be involvement of the valuation expert for setting up the buy-out price.

It is unpleasant to spend any of your resources, be it time, energy or cash, on correcting the initial mistake. Important to keep in mind though is that the longer you delay it, the costlier it will be and that, in the long run, correcting the mistake the right way is almost always cheaper than correcting it the wrong way (or not at all). If you feel that you might need help anywhere, go and get it.

Make it binding

Hopefully you did manage to correctly identify the issue and come to an agreement on how to solve it. Whether it is a buy-out and cofounder exiting, adjusting your equity split or adding (missing parts of) a cofounding agreement, do make sure you have it documented, in writing and signed by all involved parties.

For the cofounder exit, it is important to include in the buy-out agreement that all intellectual property developed during the cooperation remains with the company and clearly state which limitations (non-compete, confidentiality) are binding for the leaving cofounder.

For adjusting the equity split, depending on the form of your company, the individual situation of involved cofounders and in which country your company is operating, there might be different tax and legal consequences on how you do it, whether by shares redistribution between the partners or by issuing of new shares. Given all the variables, it is unfortunately not possible to come up with generic advice, so you will need to discuss this with your lawyer and accountant to avoid further unpleasant surprises. Prevention is always cheaper than cure.

Do not repeat the same mistake

Hopefully you got the chance to fix whatever it was in a way that your business can continue and flourish, without spending years in court rooms and suffering damaged relationships. The real cases of bad and publicised business partner fall-outs are plenty. The ones that managed to find a solution are probably not getting so much publicity, happy to be unknown and prosperous.

For continuing:

Keep your partnership agreement alive by regular reviews of any changes that might be required and using it as a map for future strategic decisions. Do invest the time and resources by spending time with your team. Get regular counselling sessions to help you get the best out of your team. And do not ignore any (even baby) elephants in the room as soon as you see them.

If your team decides to add a new additional cofounder, take it through steps 2-7.

If a cofounder is leaving, your solid cofounding agreement will govern on how to deal with is. Remember to also sign the separation/termination agreement with the leaving cofounder.

For terminating:

If your business partnership will not continue in the future, hopefully you managed to find an agreement on how to terminate it. And my hope for you is also that you learned from the mistakes and if you have a future business project, the fact that you did make a mistake in the past will not discourage you from considering a business partnership in the future. Sometimes we learn best by doing, and making mistakes is part of it.

 ## Checklist

- I corrected what was needed by reaching a new agreement with the cofounding team.

- I documented it/updated it in our cofounder agreement.

CHAPTER 11:

CLOSING REMARKS

Together we are stronger. With the exception that partnership is really not for you, I would always recommend team work – you can bounce ideas, overcome your individual bias, benefit from the critical view of others. The demanding entrepreneurial path does not feel so lonely, you get additional resources, hands, skills, access to networks and the benefits of combined perseverance and motivation.

> **"Like long legs and Loubotins, we were good on our own, but oh so much better together."**
>
> Patty Soffer

It is not a secret that strong teams are stronger than the stronger individual; what seems as a secret though is how to make business partnerships work. Looking at the staggering failure rate, there must be a better way. And I believe there is. It comes with awareness about the risks, knowledge about which options you have and the ability to learn from the mistakes of others.

As Jim Collins made a great point in his book *Good to Great,* great leaders first ask the question who, then what: 'In fact, leaders of companies that go from good to great start not with "where" but with "who." They start by getting the right people on the bus, the wrong people off the bus, and the right people in the right seats. And they stick with that discipline – first the people, then the direction – no matter how dire the circumstances.'[26] And I believe this is not only applicable for taking companies from good to great but also to taking ideas to make companies.

Many entrepreneurs devote a lot of their resources to developing the right idea, the right product, the right service, the right business plan – the list goes on. And yes, all of that is needed. However, the right team is the base with which you can build all of that and very often this aspect is underestimated with the cofounding decisions being rushed.

So be wise. Follow the map – there is one. The Seven Cofounding Steps provide a structured guideline to help you do all that. There are no 100% guarantees, but there are safer ways.

"Knowledge is power."

Francis Bacon

---

26 Collins, J. (2001). Good to great: why some companies make the leap... and others don't. London: Random House

And remember, '...entrepreneurship is a risky and heroic activity, necessary for growth or even the mere survival of the economy.'[27] Entrepreneurs are taking economic, social, career and psychological risk to create new companies, jobs, products, services and value. 'The amazing fact is that entrepreneurs and innovators and businesses have turned luxuries that not even kings could afford into low-priced everyday items' in our everyday lives. 'The entrepreneur is an explorer who travels into uncharted territory and opens up new routes along which we will all be travelling pretty soon.'[28]

So go out and explore. Preferably with a cofounding team that will win and last. You know how now.

> **"The people who are crazy enough to think they can change the world are the ones who do."**
>
> Rob Siltanen

27 Taleb, N. N. (2014). Antifragile: things that gain from disorder. New York: Random House Trade Paperbacks
28 Norberg, J. (2017, July 30). Entrepreneurs Are the Heroes of the World. Retrieved from: https://object.cato.org/sites/cato.org/files/pubs/pdf/catosletterv5n1.pdf

ABOUT THE AUTHOR

With one successful and one failed cofounding experience behind her, Jana Nevrlka has spent the past five years learning what's required to build better business partnerships and applying that knowledge to helping cofounders build successful businesses.

Combining her legal and business background with her entrepreneurial experience, Jana writes and speaks extensively on the subject, works as a cofounding mentor for a number of startup accelerators and organises a knowledge sharing platform called the Swiss Startups Club. In addition to all that, Jana coordinates the development of dynamic equity split templates in Europe.

Notes:

Questions for Rami -
What is your motivation
for coming on board?

Please Read Business Plan
together.
map the gap.

60/40

Buy/Sell: I own 60%
if something happens to
me it will go to _____
you will buy my portion
out from my family if
no-one wants to come on
board.
Is same for you
If you want out whats
your expectation of me

Notes:

When we start making
more than 50,000/ year
we can decide to take
some out @ that point

Expense sheet:
What I put in pre-
Romi and after
- what she's put in

Include in expense sheet
- Rent for kitchen

Capital Costs, Fixed Cost

Sales Projection. What is
current profit margin

Notes:

Sc. I

Fixed Cost → (bottles) 5000

Variable cost △ w production

inputs
kitchen
~~bottles~~
labels

Vart 500

100/m
↓

~~revenue~~

100 x price
20 x retail = x
80 x whole = y

T. revenue = x+y
$400
$400
.40

$160

$~~800~~

$~~840~~

Notes:

Notes:

Notes: